To the Melurkedee people, the original inhabitants, who fed themselves from this ground for at least 42,000 years, and to those farmers and custodians of land around the globe who are dedicated to soil.

The Commons

Matthew Evans

Photography by Alan Benson

Hardie Grant BOOKS SBS

Contents

Introduction

It's all about potential. Every bit of land has the potential to be something, be it wilderness, or an ornamental garden, or a farm. We bought our farm because it showed promise.

The grass was emerald and chest high when we invested our money in 70 acres of the Huon Valley. This grass was the glorious result of an ungrazed spring and decent soil. We thought, if we can grow grass, then we can grow other things. An old timer told us the woody slope to one side is called Bandicoot Hill, because the soil's so poor you couldn't grow bandicoots on it. But fertility, the good topsoil, moves downhill, and this little patch of Tasmania – the sides of our valley floor – was catching that fertility before it disappeared down the creek.

Where once there were paddocks and a neglected but ancient apple orchard, now there is the start of a verdant mixed farm. Pigs and chooks range. Cattle roam, goats ramble and there's a whole corner that's devoted to a market garden. Even the old orchard has been given a new lease on life, with the old red delicious trees grafted over to 27 different types of apple.

This land, after being inhabited for about 42,000 years, first by the Melurkedee people, then later by European migrants, has always seen change. It's fed people for a very, very long time. Our hope is that it can feed people for another few thousand years. That's the big picture, the view from a long way off. We will only be here for a moment, in historical terms; we're caretakers of this patch of soil for just a jot in time.

I got into farming for all the wrong reasons. It was all about self interest; as a glutton, I simply wanted the best-tasting food on my plate. And as a writer, in a less selfish way, I've always been trying to get people, ordinary, everyday people, to understand that they can get good food on their plates too.

But now I see our duty also revolves around community. We build communities of microbes under the soil that feed our plants and make them taste more like vegetables and fruit should. More intensely of themselves. We grow a mixed bag of things so we don't deplete the soil of nutrients, and constantly feed these subterranean and plant communities with minerals and amendments. Because we don't like the poisons used in conventional farming, we have created a community of insects that form a new kind of harmony in the garden. And above, the garden birds come and go, sometimes taking the harvest but mostly just forming the top tier of the animal kingdom, sometimes eating those insects and, all the time, rounding out our modest farming ecosystem.

When we set up the farm as a commercial restaurant, we started hiring people, and this community has buoyed us and made us stronger and better at what we do. The people who have helped build Fat Pig Farm have come with noble aims and strong backs and good grace, and this community has made us resilient, but also made us even more aware of the importance of those souls who live around us.

What's more, there's another community. It's made up of those who join us at the table. Each week, the dynamic changes, the energy driven by diners who bring their own vivaciousness and life experiences to the event. And it's this community that has surprised us the most, because while trying to capture a moment in time on the plate, we've also captured a moment in time in the room. All those people who dine at our table bring countless generations with them in their spirit, and break bread and make joy over platters of shared farm produce.

And so, this book is about the commons. What we share in common, what we feel in common, what we can do in common.

We see ourselves sharing in a common past with those who walked and fed themselves on this patch of land. We share a common future with those around us. And it's for the common good that we are nurturing our soil, because this land is only ours for the moment. We may own this land, but it will outlast us, and our child's children.

The changes, in the mere eight years since we bought the place, seem slow. When you pace the ground daily, it really is like watching grass grow. Not just grass, but trees and shrubs and orchards, and wildlife corridors. We bought our farm because we had an inkling of its past, and saw its possible future.

As we farm, we watch as the seasons rotate, slowly, through their inexorable cycles. Each period means we're more attuned, wiser to nature's wants, even as we become greyer and slower on the ground. I wish I'd started farming earlier in life. Like I wish I'd started a family earlier. Like I wish I'd learned to skydive and weld and sing. You have to start sometime, though, and our attitude is that we at least started. My partner Sadie and I have been giving farming a crack for more than a decade now, first at a little farm over the hill and now here. And yes, we make mistakes. But the only people who don't make mistakes are those who don't make anything.

I met a brother and sister who grew up here. And by here, I mean on this exact patch of dirt. They had an orchard, a large garden, grazed animals on what we now call Fat Pig Farm. They milked a cow and their mum sold milk and butter from their farmhouse. Oh, how the rules have changed. Few can milk two cows these days and meet the regulations. I love the fact we're continuing tradition, even if it does mean paperwork and regulation and pasteurisation. Cows have been milked here since cows arrived. Families have grown large and strong on milk from cows that grazed this farm. We have but a moment in time to live and care for this land, as did the former owners and long-term Indigenous custodians. What we do has resonance for the past, and the future.

When we see old photos, it reminds us of what we have done, not what is yet to come. Without photos, as I lope around these 70 acres, an hour south of Hobart, I see the vision, the long game. I look at a sapling and see its long-term possibilities. You see a knee-high olive tree, I see oil and cured olives and a mature grove there for generations to have picnics in. I wish for a pin oak of some magnificence to fill the view for my grandchildren, while all that sits there now is a head-high tree. I want for more fertile soil, for less erosion, and build swales (old-fashioned drains) that ring some of the slopes. I may not see their full effect in my lifetime.

They say some people are consumed by the lack of progress to what they foresee, more concerned by the way they fall short of their visions than what they have achieved. Maybe we are more like that. Or maybe we're just impatient, wanting results even if results – when it comes to the land – can take hundreds, if not thousands, of years to come to fruition. Other people, be they visitors to our farm or those who we work with, see what we have done, not what is yet to come.

We're quite proud of what we're building, and what we've built. I do hope others like what they see.

Winter

Wood fires
Snuggly wrapped kids
Naked trees
Whisky
Broccoli
Frosty mornings
Root vegetables
Pie baking
Mud
Salami making
Beanies and gloves
Long sleeps
Hot soup
Fog
More mud
Parkin
Woolly jumpers
Mulled cider

•

Recipes

Sometimes it hits with a thwack. Sometimes winter creeps in as silently as frost.

The light angles in, the sun only 21 degrees above the horizontal. It's this winter light that defines us. The low light gives a warm glow to everything, when the sun shines. The low light slows down the growth of our crops as they struggle to photosynthesise the sun's rays. This dreamy-looking warm light isn't enough to warm the soil, and so things in the garden move slower in winter.

The same, to some extent, can be said for us. We try to wake later and retire, at least to the fireplace, earlier. We have fewer urgent chores when there's rain falling and water in the dams and in the soil. The harvest in the garden is quicker. The pigs are happier; for this British breed, the Wessex Saddleback, our winter is drier and warmer than their origins. It's like the tropics for them compared to the UK.

At times, we move faster. There's less lingering in the dairy when the frost bites and the fog rolls in. We move to warm up, tramping up and down the hills with more vigour than in the hot days of summer. I am usually found, hands plunged deep in pockets, leaning into the wind if it's cold, or finding precious spots of sunshine to thaw out in on sunny days.

At night, I brave the cold before bed to gaze skywards and admire the heavens, so emblazoned with the light of far-off suns, always hoping to spot the majestic southern lights, the Aurora Australis.

Winter is transformative. The cold kills a bunch of pests in the garden. The cool nights allow us to grow our crops with the right amount of flavour. The restorative nature of winter is an antidote to the prolonged days of summer for the farmers as well as the farm. It lets us look inwards. To reflect more. To plan more. And to play catch-up on a lot of chores.

Winter in the Huon, where we live, means mud. It means the occasional frost. Winter is about hunkering down over steaming bowls of soup, warming stews, hot pies and red wine. We do winter well in Tasmania, a period of prolonged cold that marks us out, and defines our wardrobe. It is a true winter, where beauty abounds, providing a clear contrast to the seasons that border and oppose it. If you haven't seen the clear skies, the boundless stars, felt the sting of the rain on your face in a Huon Valley winter, you've only half lived.

The Winter

We sow our winter crops from December on, but most go into the ground in February, when the summer crops are often still just ready to harvest. The long, slow ripening and growing times, as the light drops and the soil cools, make for really intense flavour. Frost sweetens lots of things, but in particular root vegetables like parsnip, and brassicas such as broccoli and kale. There's no fruit from the garden, just a few apples in the fridge, and preserves and the like to choose from.

Harvest

June.
Kohlrabi, broccoli, fennel, leeks, Jerusalem artichokes, spigarello, kale, nettle.

July.
Cabbage, oca. Loads of greens, including silverbeet (Swiss chard) and other chard-like greens. Onions. Last chance for roasted carrots. Parsnips. The last of the brussels sprouts. Cauliflower.

August.
Swedes, turnips, broccoli raab. The last of the big brassicas: broccoli, cabbage, kohlrabi. Still have kale and silverbeet, parsley and dill. Salsify, beetroot (beets).

2
JUNE

Winter is upon us. The days have shrunk in length, the nights are long. Cold seeps in when a door is left ajar. The doona beckons early, and holds me late. I relish the quiet indoor times, the solid sleep of the weary, warm underneath the covers, a window cracked so the cool, fresh air – snuffled by a nose, just a nose, that braves the space above the covers – cleanses my senses.

I do get up. And chores, jobs that invigorate the soul, I do. Today it was a seamless weaning of slips (what farmers call piglets). That's seamless if by that you mean two piglets doing the 200-metre dash around the corner and into the garden, not into their new paddocks. A pig can find an open gate, an opportunity, at every turn. These two slips have found the mother lode: the bountiful market garden, where a kilometre of garden beds beckon.

Soon – after minimal damage and frantic rounding up – they're back with their siblings. I take a photo to record the response of these piglets to weaning, the first separation from mum, where five of them are sleeping, and one looks up at the camera, with careless indifference, not even bothering to stand.

Moving pigs isn't like herding cats. That would be easy. Moving pigs is like trying to round up a bunch of preschoolers using cabbage as the motivator. Sure, they're interested in food. They're motivated by it. But they spend most of their days testing the boundaries, and the moment they get a sense of freedom, food ceases to be of interest. Particularly boring 'good-for-you' food of the kind a parent would provide. No, dirt looks more inviting. Or weeds. Or a whole garden full of goodies. A stray butterfly is more to their liking than staying as a mob, or moving where they're supposed to. Owning pigs is a lesson in patience. In persuasion. Moving pigs with a significant other is a good way to have a row, so it's usually done alone, or with someone who works here, rather than someone you share a home with.

As the cold bites, we start to move hay around. Hay for the goats, which for the moment are locked in the top paddock. Hay for the cattle, usually a long way from the road head. Our farm, a kilometre long, is mostly accessible only by foot at this time of year. We load the top shed with hay in the summer, then it's only a 100-metre lug with bales on your back. This pacing the land keeps us very much in tune with the soil. With the advancement and retreat of weeds. With the feel of our earth. But some days I feel the weight of a bale of hay more than others. It helps when the days are nice. Most are.

We are in the midst of calm days, in contrast to the storms of past weeks. Warm afternoons where I want to linger in the garden, and days when I struggle to get our guests back to the dining room after a Friday feast. I understand their reluctance. On days like this, there's nowhere else I'd rather be than pacing the paddocks.

The bush tucker garden is starting to take shape. The fencing yet to be finished, the wallabies hungry. The fruit trees are nude. The leaves long gone, the fruit – apart from the apples, of which there are some in cold storage – just a memory. A fond memory.

There's leftover bread. Again. Often I make a kumquat-scented bread and butter pudding, but there's a different plan for this loaf, whiter than we normally bake, and perfect for another use. We make a wicked bread sauce, inspired by the walnut paste of Georgia: garlicky and sharp with lemon zest, to go with Jerusalem artichokes. There's pork fat to use up, ready for a hot water pastry or the like.

We await the bulk of the rain. I've left it too late to get a water tank for the top of the Hedley paddock; the ground's too slippery for driving on. I want, as fits our philosophy, a metal water tank that will break down sooner rather than later, galvanised steel rather than plastic. Plastic would only become our descendants' problem.

Last week we had cracker night, where a local farmer opens his paddocks and his barn to the hordes, and the licensed are allowed to let off a few fireworks. These occasional family outings, where we see our farming and other friends, bind us to the community. And thus it was so: rugged up in beanies and gumboots, dressed for a cold night next to a big bonfire, we sipped hot spiced apple juice. There was a barbecue with chops and patties. Platters of winter veg, mostly grown by the person who brought it. And a child too excited for words.

20
JUNE

In the market garden, we're just growing vegetables. It's not rocket science; it's way more complicated. We're dealing with the ecosystem under the soil, the ecosystem in the soil, the ecosystem above the soil and the weather, which is so complicated. Growing good food is this glorious miracle, turning soil, air, water and sunlight into things we can enjoy.

Firewood. It's the perennial problem. What wood? Where to stack it? Can we avoid double or triple handling it? It fires our ovens and flavours our food. We use it for heat, for grilling. Wood is the original sustainable fuel source. You can burn a tree and grow a tree. It's much harder to grow natural gas or petrol. Every year we go through the angst of buying or cutting wood, working out months in advance what we'll need, and how best to store it so that

it becomes, and stays, dry. Outside, in our climes, the wood still absorbs moisture, even if it's under cover and gets the sun. It takes a few days indoors to really dry out, to get to the point where it flames without smoke. Firewood not looked after, bought too late, or stacked too poorly, can make you suffer. It's firewood that wards off the cold, and so we take the getting of it very seriously indeed.

Rarely, the farm is submerged in fog. A thick, wet white bank of cloud that cuts us off from the world, just letting the sounds drift in. Wedged between the hills and the river, our valley fills with it. We watch as fog drifts down, like a cloudy river, seemingly draining out into the sea. But somewhere, upriver from here, the fog is being made almost as quickly as it departs, the blanket at first feeling joyously snug overhead, but by mid-afternoon starting to become a little more stifling than comforting.

It lifts late on two days this week. A drape of cosiness that some see as bitter cold. Perhaps they've not been to Europe in winter, or North America, and seen what cold really feels like?

This week, we're inundated with cauliflower. There's a bounty of kohlrabi. Sweet, gleaming fennel. Even some salsify, the black-skinned variety that some call oyster fruit for its gentle, elegant, almost oyster-like taste.

It has rained. Chucked it down, really, and the paddocks are wet underfoot. Kellie's Bog, the spot in the paddocks just outside the restaurant that our cook Kellie McChesney got so stuck in that she came out of her boots the year we opened the restaurant, is starting to get mucky again. The winter creek is living up to its name, running fast after we had more than 50 mm of rain on the weekend.

8 JULY

The price of summer is winter. The wind whips up from the west. It's about 6°C, the sun comes and goes, but mostly goes. The rain comes in bursts, and the land, long ago waterlogged, is no longer able to absorb a drop that falls from the heavens. There's next to no evaporation, and won't be for a couple of months, despite the shortest day now being but a memory, even if it was just a fortnight ago. Glorious winter. Incredible winter. The season that separates the hardy from the foolhardy; those who love Tassie from those who love to visit.

We pay for the summer bounty on days like this. It's this long, cold winter that gives the raspberries their oomph. Long days graced with honeyed, tree-ripened apricots are more appreciated if you've lived through the dark of winter. While now we can enjoy cauliflower, and salsify, and brussels sprouts – food that suits the season when snow caps the peaks – it's the winter that intensifies the summer. There's obviously the joy that comes when the weather breaks and warmth returns with the sun, but it's the cold of our winters that breaks the cycle of pests and imbues the stone fruit with flavour; that ability is what makes where we live so delectable.

Not that I'm in any hurry for summer. It will come soon enough. For now, there's joy when the carrots have spent weeks in the frost.

The leaves of the greens are suddenly sweeter, too. Our parsnips reach their peak in the hard, cold depths of the year, not so stingy on the tongue as those grown in easier climes.

Our cow Elsie has started to wean her calf Lily after nearly ten months. The grass is growing where the wallaby-proof fence was recently finished. The pigs have moved nearer the house and, while I wasn't really keen on them being near home at first, afraid they'd break out and get into the garden, I get a kick out of seeing pigs outside the back door. It makes it feel like a farmhouse again, like we're smallholders just growing what we need, rather than running a small restaurant on 70 acres.

The new dairy cow, Florence, is due to arrive any day. Another jersey to join the existing herd. Florence will graze alongside our other jersey, Myrtle, and the guernsey, Elsie. She's coming from friends of ours over in the next valley, who have come to the sad realisation they can no longer milk every day. Taking her on feels like a privilege: a cow who can be hand-milked or machine-milked. A cow who shares her precious gift with us each day, and one who was very much part of her previous family. The micro dairy we run is a folly, but one I've pursued. I love the way milk is transformed. The way grass can be converted to milk, the milk to butter, or cheese, or clotted cream. I like being around dairy cows, I like watching over their wellbeing, talking to them when nobody is watching. Sensing their moods, their joys, their pain. I once read a book on a micro dairy in the US, where the farmer wasn't sure if the soft, brown-eyed animal he fell for was incredibly clever, or incredibly dumb. The longer I spend with mine, I'm equally bewildered. It's easy to discard their manner for naivety or lack of brain. But then they'll do something that seems to speak of far deeper thought, of far deeper understanding.

We milk because we think the product is better. But the rules around running the dairy, the paperwork, the way what we do is judged as though we're about to start milking 1000 head, not two or three; those rules are grinding. I've often wondered why there are virtually no farm-based restaurants that grow the vegies, rear the meat *and* milk the cows or goats. Now I know why. You just wouldn't bother unless you believed in it. For the cost, the hassle, the time, it'd be far easier to just go and buy a few litres of milk. Especially when dairy farmers have been screwed to the wall with prices.

Brussels sprouts form hard against the stem of the plant, like mini cabbages tucked between the stems of the plants' leaves.

Frost sweetens the winter harvest.

14
JULY

The flags are flying, the bacon baked beans are cooked, the food van has been shifted to the paddocks outside the Apple Shed in Grove, about 20 minutes up the road. We've put feathers in our top hats and put on face paint for the Huon Valley Mid Winter Festival. Run by the very brilliant Willie Smith's, the big local cidery, this is a celebration of all things apple. They hold a wassailing festival, where cider is poured on the apple trees to bring forth good spirits for next year's harvest. More to the point, they put on good music and good food and good cider so we locals, and a lot of non-locals, it must be said, can celebrate our cooler months.

The middle of winter can be a time of hunkering down. A time when we work less during the days, and relish the long nights, complete with mulled cider and whisky and warming fires. Locals still socialise, but less so. We hibernate a bit more, yet when a festival like this bobs up, we're well kitted out for the weather and well and truly ready for the dancing. Girls in pretty, multilayered frocks wear gumboots on their feet to ward off the mud. Men in long, woollen coats can be seen gesticulating madly during conversation near the bonfire. A team of archers set fire to the burning man, a giant grinning effigy built of ploughshares and tractor parts. Fire lights our lives and ignites our passions, none more so than the pursuit of food.

There's mud. And more mud. I live in gumboots, wellington boots my English-born mother would call them. I live in my wellies, because even when there's no mud, the grass will drench your shoes. It is often wet from dew. Occasionally, not often, from frost. Sometimes from rain. It doesn't matter the cause, because it stays wet most days, because there's not enough warmth in the air, or height in the sun, to dry it completely. Lots of Australian farmers think of mud as money in the bank. Mud means moisture when so often the land is desiccated. Right now, it just feels like mud.

16 AUGUST

Elsie is back to her herd, and out of the milking routine. In fact, we're not milking at all for a couple of months. Stopping milking a cow is like when a child goes to school for the first time and leaves the house without you for a change. Yes, you do look forward to the freedom, but jeez, you miss them. I miss my early morning ritual with the cows, the warmth of the bodies in the cool of the dawn. Their musky, grassy breath blowing misty in the low light. The lazy chewing of the cud as they meander from the dairy up the laneways back to their paddocks. I often think I missed my calling in life. I think I'd enjoy being a cow herder full time. I love watching their ambling. I find incomparable pleasure watching cows ruminating. I enjoy grappling with what it must mean to be a cow; the herd dynamics, the desire for routine, the inscrutability of their expressions.

The mud is insane this year. There are, for the first time in seven years, springs where there were none. Burbling up in paddocks. Seeping out in garden beds. We have driveways that feel like trampolines. There's even standing water on the slopes, puddles in the middle of a hillside, bodies of water that seem to defy gravity.

Tasmania is blessed with all kinds of weather. Today, that weather includes winds that sound like jumbos taking off. They scuttle past at over 100 km an hour, disturbing our sleep, rattling the roof. The house shakes so much that the furniture squeaks in the night with the gusts. All our flues have sprung leaks. The hot water system has shuddered loose. The chimney has blown over in the last big gusts. At times like this, we bunker down with mugs of tea and bowls of rice pudding. We awake to find things still in place. Remarkably, there's nothing much to see, not a tree down. Not a lot is left loose, but what is hasn't – thankfully – become a projectile. Just some tarps blown around in the garden, and the poor brussels sprouts, long and leggy, top-heavy at the end of their days, are stooped by the big blow.

Life's a cycle. Trimmings from kohlrabi and cabbage help to fatten the pigs.

28 AUGUST

The late winter isn't really late winter. In other parts of the globe, the seasons are counted from the solstice, the longest or shortest days. So winter, if we were in other climes, would be measured from the 22nd of June to the 21st of September. That didn't make much sense when I lived in the city. The weird mid-month date, seemingly arbitrary and confusing. But now, when we watch the far hills for signs of thaw in the snow and feel the chill of the earth beneath our toes, it makes more sense. For two months the days have got longer, but the light belies the intensity of the cold. It will be a month before we really start to feel the warmth.

We have goats, meat goats, but we're too afraid to kill them. We joke about eating the goats if they don't eat the blackberry bushes. And boy, are they eating the blackberries. What's more, we feel they haven't really had the chance to settle in, and Sadie and our son, Hedley, are naming them. Names: they make taking any animal to the slaughterhouse even more challenging. While they are doing what we wanted them to do, I'll get meat from a farm on the other side of town.

As we near spring, and the place is as green as it can be (if still fringed with mud), I remember the importance of bud burst. The time when the new leaves of deciduous plants yawn open, and the sap, very slowly at first, starts to run again. This moment is the first sign of nature waking up, the glorious day when you know that it won't, like Narnia, be winter forever. And it's an important moment in the biology of all our fruiting trees. Bud burst!

Of course, I missed it again. Most years the quince get a jump on us, sneaking out buds before we can spray them with a bit of copper. The copper stops leaf rust, meaning the plant has way more healthy leaves, and hence energy to put into growing and flowering and making plump, fragrant fruit. The quince are sprayed. But perhaps too late for the autumn crop, still so long away it seems almost impossible to countenance.

Much closer is the annual pig day. The day we turn a pig, or this year, two over two days, into all our cured meats for the coming year. I've been feeding acorns to two pigs. For three weeks they've been finished on a diet mostly of these nuts, and they look magnificent. It's not the long, slow finishing that Spain's famed pata negra get before being turned into that incredible ham, *jamon iberico de bellota*. Those Iberian black-footed pigs spend months under cork and gall oaks, foraging for acorns of their own accord.

My acorns took a few hours to rake up under a tree at the local childcare centre. A lot of work for a 20 kg bag of pig nuts. Let's hope the result is worth the effort.

Winter, a time of tree planting, is also a time of putting up prosciutto to cure. A 140 kg pig, with legs to match, has been turned into salami and lonzo (cured loin) and pancetta and capocollo. We also managed to get 10 kg or so of fresh sausages. It can take a village to find ways to cure a big pig. I did it, with a bit of help from James Mele, the incomparable sixth-generation salami maker from Victoria's The Meat Room, and Brett, our apprentice, over two days.

The proof, they say, is in the eating. And the proof with this prosciutto will be a year in the making.

Apple and Orange Tart

Serves 6

I was given this recipe by the people who lived next door to me in Wales when I was growing up. As a visitor from Australia in my twenties, I'd hitch-hiked through the snow to meet them and we were talking food at the kitchen table when a man knocked on the back door and offered us two pheasants. I gutted and cooked the pheasant, and I did a rough job on both counts. The tart that they made, however, was simple and delicious.

whipped cream, to serve

Pastry

125 g (4½ oz/½ cup) butter, softened

60 g (2 oz) caster (superfine) sugar

250 g (9 oz/1⅔ cups) plain (all-purpose) flour

2 free-range egg yolks

icing (confectioners') sugar, for dusting

Filling

1 large orange

180 g (6½ oz) caster (superfine) sugar

3 free-range eggs, beaten

2 large green cooking apples, washed and cored

In a food processor, cream the butter with the sugar until light. Pulse in the flour and then the egg yolks until just combined. Scrape out of the machine and press into a ball, then cover with plastic wrap. Rest for about 1 hour in the fridge.

When ready, roll the pastry out between sheets of plastic wrap or baking paper, to line a 35 × 12 cm (14 × 4¾ in) flan tin, or equivalent tin. Rest it in the fridge for a further 30 minutes.

Preheat the oven to 220°C (430°F).

While the pastry is resting, make the filling. Grate the zest from the orange, then squeeze the juice and strain. Place the zest and juice in a mixing bowl, then add the sugar and eggs and mix well. Grate the apple, squeeze to drain excess moisture and then stir the flesh into the orange and sugar mixture.

Pour the filling into the pastry case and bake for 10 minutes, then reduce the oven temperature to 200°C (400°F) and continue baking for 15–25 minutes, or until set.

Remove from the oven and allow to cool before dusting with icing sugar. Serve at room temperature, perhaps with a dollop of cream, though it doesn't usually need it.

Winter food should be like getting embraced in one great big hug.

Apple Cider–battered Cauliflower Fritters

Serves 10

Simple cauliflower becomes a must-have snack with drinks when encased in a fragrant cider batter.

1 large cauliflower head

plain (all-purpose) flour, for dusting

Cider Batter

200 g (7 oz/1⅓ cups) self-raising flour

½ teaspoon salt, plus extra for sprinkling

1 teaspoon ground cumin

1 teaspoon ground coriander

1 teaspoon ground black pepper

½ teaspoon ground turmeric

1 teaspoon dried mint (a good Turkish-style one is ideal)

300 ml (10 fl oz) apple cider

olive oil, for deep-frying

lemon wedges, to serve

Cut the cauliflower into even, bite-sized florets, working from the stem outwards. Place in a bowl and lightly dust with plain flour, then set aside.

To prepare the batter, mix the self-raising flour, salt, spices and mint in a mixing bowl, stirring just a couple of times to evenly combine, then slowly pour in the cider and whisk until the batter is smooth.

Pour 3 cm (1¼ in) oil into a deep saucepan or wok and heat to around 180°C (350°F). To check the temperature, place a wooden skewer in the oil and, when it sizzles, it's nice and hot.

Dust any excess flour off the cauliflower pieces and, using your fingers, dip one at a time into the batter, tapping on the side of the bowl to remove any surplus, then carefully lower the floret into the hot oil. Fry in small batches so as not to overcrowd the pan and please, try not to deep-fry your fingers.

Use a slotted spoon to turn the fritters over a couple of times until golden brown, then remove from the oil and drain on paper towel.

Serve each batch as they're cooked. You need to eat them straight away, while the batter is still crisp, sprinkled with extra salt and served with lemon wedges for squeezing over. Continue until all the cauliflower is cooked and consumed.

Salt and Vinegar Oca

Serves 6

This is probably my favourite vegetable snack over the cooler months. Oca are New Zealand yams – a red- to orange-coloured subterranean tuber with Michelin man–style rolls in the skin. It's a remarkably delicious little thing that needs little more than a good roasting and top-notch vinegar to match its natural sweetness. To us, they're like a healthier, better-tasting version of that lip-smacking treat I loved as a kid: salt and vinegar chips.

500 g (1 lb 2 oz) oca, cleaned well, no need to peel

3–4 tablespoons olive oil

2 tablespoons white-wine vinegar

Preheat the oven to 200°C (400°F).

Rub the oca with enough olive to coat them liberally, then place in a roasting tin and cook in the oven for about 20–25 minutes, tossing every now and then until soft.

As soon as they come out of the oven, toss in the hot pan with the vinegar, then finish with lashings of salt. Serve with toothpicks, as a snack before dinner, or just because.

Roasted Cauliflower with Walnuts and Yoghurt

Serves 6 as a side dish

The flavour of cauliflower is sensational in lots of ways, but when it's fried or roasted until brown, it brings out all kinds of extra goodness.

1 cauliflower head, cut into florets

3–4 tablespoons olive oil

200 g (7 oz) plain yoghurt

4 roasted garlic cloves

1–2 tablespoons extra-virgin olive oil

about 100 g (3½ oz/1 cup) roasted and lightly crushed walnuts

Preheat the oven to 200°C (400°F).

Toss the cauliflower florets with enough olive oil to lightly coat, using your fingertips to spread it out evenly, then add salt and pepper to taste.

Lay the cauliflower in a roasting tin and roast, tossing occasionally, until browned. More colour is better than less. It can take quite a varying amount of time, depending on how much moisture is in the cauliflower.

Meanwhile, whisk the yoghurt with the roasted garlic, adding the extra-virgin olive oil to taste. When the cauliflower is ready, cool it a little, toss with the yoghurt and walnuts and serve. It can look a bit messy, but the flavour more than makes up for it.

Chickpeas with Roasted Cauliflower and Drained Yoghurt

Serves 4–6

I soak and simmer dried chickpeas for this, simply because they're purer and taste better. But on a day when there's less time to prepare, a tin of chickpeas, drained and rinsed, makes an okay substitute.

300 g (10½ oz) plain (ideally pot-set) yoghurt

good handful of fresh coriander (cilantro), chopped

1 cauliflower head, cut into florets

2 tablespoons olive oil, plus 1 tablespoon extra for frying

1 large onion, peeled and finely diced

½ teaspoon ground turmeric

1 teaspoon ground cumin

300 g (10½ oz) cooked chickpeas

handful of flat-leaf (Italian) parsley, roughly chopped

lemon wedges, to serve

Line a colander with a piece of muslin (cheesecloth), or a clean disposable cloth and place it over a bowl. Tip in the yoghurt and drain well until relatively thick – transfer it to the fridge if draining for more than 2 hours. When ready, stir in a good pinch of salt and the chopped coriander.

Preheat the oven to 220°C (430°F).

Toss the cauliflower with the olive oil and some salt and pepper in a roasting tin and roast until brown, turning every now and then to cook evenly.

While the cauli cooks, heat the extra oil in a large frying pan over a medium heat and fry the onion well until soft. Turn the heat right down, add the turmeric and cumin and continue to fry for about 30 seconds, or 1 minute, so that the spices toast but don't scorch. If you're worried about the spices burning, quickly splash in a little water to arrest the cooking. Toss in the chickpeas and turn to coat evenly in the oil and spices. Mix the chickpeas with the cauliflower and parsley, adding a little more oil if it's too dry.

Serve warm or at room temperature with the drained yoghurt and perhaps some lemon for squeezing.

Bresaola and Witlof Salad with Boiled Lemon

Serves 4

Bresaola is air-dried beef, and it's really good as a change from prosciutto. Here, I've made a sharp, lightly bitter salad and used it to match the fragrance and saltiness of the meat. You can serve as I do here, as an entrée or as part of a shared platter, or even cut the meat into strips and toss it in to make more of a mixed salad.

1 whole lemon, scrubbed (or use fresh lemon juice and the rind of 1 preserved lemon)

½ teaspoon salt

1 bay leaf

4 chicory (witlof/endive)

2 tablespoons finely shredded flat-leaf (Italian) parsley

generous pinch of sugar

2–3 tablespoons extra-virgin olive oil

100 g (3½ oz) bresaola, finely sliced

Juice the lemon and set aside the juice. If you're using preserved lemon, you don't need to do the next boiling bit. Take the two halves of rind and place in a small saucepan with enough water to cover, then add the salt and bay leaf. Place over a high heat and bring to the boil, cover, and turn down to a simmer. Boil for about 30 minutes, or until tender. Cool, remove any pith and slice the rind into thin strips.

To make the salad, slice the chicory about 2–3 mm (⅛ in) thick across the leaves, discarding the hard core. Toss with the parsley and half the sliced lemon rind. Dress the leaves with about 1 tablespoon lemon juice, the sugar and 2 tablespoons olive oil and some salt and pepper. Remember: the meat is salty, so don't overdo it. (If there's any leftover lemon juice you can keep it for other uses.) Toss gently to combine and taste.

Lay the bresaola out on plates or a platter, place the salad in the middle of the plates, and add some more lemon rind and olive oil. Serve immediately.

Cider-baked Fennel

Serves 4 as a side dish

Good fennel can be served raw, slivered in salads, or quickly seared in a pan. At times, however, when we have more of it, we like to braise it in the oven. We use cider, because we're in an apple-growing valley, but you could mix it up with white wine, or even water with some extra flavourings such as lemon zest and juice.

2 large fennel bulbs

1 medium onion, peeled and finely sliced

2 fresh thyme sprigs

1 bay leaf

125 ml (4 fl oz/½ cup) dry cider

Preheat the oven to 200°C (400°F).

Clean the fennel bulbs by stripping the tops off, then trim with a sharp knife or potato peeler to remove any dried or brown outside bits. Cut the root off to trim it close to the bulb, too.

Cut the fennel bulbs in half, then cut each half into four, through the root. Lay evenly over the base of a 1 litre (34 fl oz/4 cup) casserole dish, or similar. Top with the sliced onion, thyme and bay leaf, and splash on the cider. Add salt and pepper to taste. Cover the fennel with a slip of baking paper to hold in all that yummy steam as it cooks, then cover the whole tray tightly with foil.

Bake in the oven for about 45 minutes to 1 hour, or until the fennel is tender. Serve warm with cooked meats, or cool.

Roasted Cabbage with Spicy Calabrese Salami

Serves 6

Just like it sounds. Good cabbage, sweetened by the winter frost. Good salami, roasted in the oven to get it to yield some of that fat, and the result is just deliciousness on the plate.

150 g (5½ oz) Calabrese (spicy) salami, cut into quarters or halved lengthways, then cut into 2 cm (¾ in) wide chunks

1 cabbage head (about 1 kg/2 lb 3 oz), outer leaves trimmed, stem and core removed, cut into chunks

2–3 tablespoons pork fat

1–2 tablespoons red or white-wine vinegar (optional)

bread, to serve

Preheat the oven to 220°C (430°F).

Pop the salami into a large roasting tin (one that will fit the cabbage later) and roast for about 5–10 minutes until the salami is starting to render fat, but does not dry out too much. Remove the salami with a slotted spoon and set aside.

Place the cabbage in the same roasting tin with the pork fat and sprinkle with a little salt (remembering that the salami will add more salt to the finished dish). Roast for about 20 minutes, or even longer, turning often to coat and cook more evenly. The hotter the better, I think, as it's great to get some brown bits on the edges.

When it's ready, toss in the salami, and return it to the oven to reheat for a minute or two. Taste for seasoning and, if it's too rich, throw in a tablespoon or two of wine vinegar to bring back to balance, then serve immediately with bread.

A Lesson in Patience

A sure-fire way to work out how patient you are is to own pigs. Pigs, god love them, are remarkably stubborn. Until they're not. They're very much their own beings, not interested in what we want. You can entice, encourage, bribe, cajole and still be left with an unmoved pig.

They say pigs are as smart as a three- to four-year-old human. Or smarter than a dog. They certainly spend all day testing the boundaries, like a three-year-old human does. And they're highly motivated by food like a toddler. Until they're not. So trying to shift a half dozen pigs into a trailer is a remarkably good way to have a blue with your partner. Sadie and I now try to move pigs with other people, or on our own, just to help remove at least one road bump in the relationship journey. That said, we've found our own peace with it now. It's a bit like the angst expressed in professional kitchens, when you forgive the shouty, sweary chef over drinks after work. What's said while moving pigs stays in the paddock.

Anyway, all of that is to say pigs are very headstrong. They have very clear personalities that we humans pick up on quite quickly. They are also endearing to have on the farm. Endlessly sociable, a pig is always playing, fighting, sleeping next to, or feeding near another pig. They experience the world through their snout. With a sense of smell several hundred times stronger than ours, their world is way more complicated than we sense it. Remove them from their current paddock, and a whole new universe opens up.

Pigs get a bad rap. Sweat like a pig? Well, pigs don't sweat, they have to wallow to control their temperature on hot days. A dirty pig? They are actually quite clean, toileting a long way from their beds, and staying relatively glossy and nice-looking unless they're stuck in dusty or muddy surrounds. Snouts in the trough? The only time I've seen my pigs behaving like politicians is when we've fed them colostrum from a newly milked cow. This must be the ultimate lolly for them and they clamour and crawl and fight to get at it. Generally, yes, they're hungry, but in a labrador kind of way. No, pigs are the butt of jokes and demeaning talk, but the animal itself is actually a bit of a noble beast.

Looking after pigs is really labour intensive. As I often say to folks thinking of getting animals on a small farm: remember, they need constant attention, like kids. But unlike kids, you can't take your pigs on holidays with you. Even if you'd like to.

Pigs can damage the ground. They destroy their water if not properly fastened down. They can turn over a paddock after a heavy lick of rain, knock over their shelter and will escape from an area that isn't properly fenced. They can bend star pickets by simply having a scratch on them, ringbark trees, pull up irrigation pipe, and generally make mischief. So why would you own pigs? Well, apart from their delightful presence, farms have pigs because they serve a purpose. They recycle lots of food we can't or won't eat, by consuming it themselves. They turn that waste vegetable matter and dairy into really good-tasting pork (a far cry from most industrial pork), which is then able to be eaten in every kind of way, from fresh to preserved for three years as prosciutto. The pig, from a cook's point of view, is delightfully, endlessly versatile.

We have pig breaking-down days on our farm, where we take the whole, very fresh pig and transform it into cured meats. Salami. Coppa. Pancetta. Bacon. Prosciutto. A day or two of labour, always in company to spread the work and the love, to transform the flesh in myriad ways. If you get bored with pork, you've run out of imagination.

Chinese Cabbage Slaw with Fennel, Hard Cheese and Walnut Oil

Serves 4–6

I use salt and sugar to soften both the texture and heat of the onion, and the flavour of the fennel. For the cabbage, giving it a little time with salt and lemon juice also helps to create a soft salad that just has a little resilience in the fatter bits of cabbage. You could put walnuts through as well, right at the end, to make this salad more of a complete meal.

1 large red onion, peeled and finely sliced

2 teaspoons salt

1½ teaspoons sugar

¼ Chinese cabbage (wombok), finely shredded

2 tablespoons lemon juice, plus extra to taste

1 fennel bulb, finely sliced

handful of flat-leaf (Italian) parsley leaves

50 g (1¾ oz) hard cheese, such as cheddar, parmesan or pecorino, finely shaved

2 tablespoons extra-virgin olive oil

1 tablespoon walnut oil

Toss the onion with ½ teaspoon salt and ½ teaspoon sugar, then set aside for 30 minutes.

While the onion sits, toss the cabbage with the lemon juice and ½ teaspoon salt and let it sit too. Do likewise with the fennel, gently tossing it with another 1 teaspoon salt and 1 teaspoon sugar, then leave to sit for 30 minutes.

When the onion is done, give it a quick rinse off and drain well. Drain the fennel well, perhaps squeezing it out a little too.

To finish the salad, toss the cabbage, onion, fennel and parsley in a large bowl, mixing evenly with your fingertips. Add the cheese and oils and mix just enough to combine. Serve straight away.

Carrots with Fermented Carrot Paste and Hazelnuts

Serves 6

This is a good recipe for making roasted carrots a dish in their own right. The complexity of the fermented carrot paste heightens the sweetness of good-quality carrots, while the snap of the hazelnuts adds a spike of richness and a contrasting crunch.

1 kg (2 lb 3 oz) young carrots, scrubbed

1–2 tablespoons olive oil

200 g (7 oz) Fermented Carrots and some of the onions (page 306)

20–30 g (¾–1 oz) butter

50 g (1¾ oz) roasted hazelnuts, lightly crushed

Preheat the oven to 200°C (400°F).

Place the fresh carrots in a roasting tin, toss with enough olive oil to coat and season well with salt and pepper. Roast for about 30 minutes, tossing occasionally to cook them more evenly. Ideally, they should get a bit of colour on them.

While the carrots cook, cut the fermented carrots and onion into rounds and simmer in a covered saucepan with just enough water to moisten – start with about 50 ml (1¾ fl oz). You want to have enough moisture so that you can purée the carrots to a paste. When soft, after about 10–15 minutes, blend with a hand-held blender or in a food processor, with the butter. Keep warm or reheat just before serving.

When the carrots are done, spread the fermented carrot paste on a platter and top with the roasted carrots, then scatter over the hazelnuts.

Swede Colcannon

Serves 6

Colcannon, that Irish dish of mashed potato with a brassica of some kind, be it kale or cabbage or the like, goes so tremendously well with rich meats like brisket, or kassler, or similar. But I can eat a plate full of it all on its own. Leftovers, fried to brown in a pan, are even better, and when it's got swede in it, well, that's dinner sorted.

500 g (1 lb 2 oz) starchy potatoes, peeled

500 g (1 lb 2 oz) butter swedes, peeled

1 teaspoon salt

100 ml (3½ fl oz) full-cream (whole) milk, or more to taste

50 g (1¾ oz) butter, or more to taste

200 g (7 oz) kale or cabbage, or even brussels sprouts, washed and shredded

Cut the potatoes and swedes into 3 cm (1¼ in) chunks. Place them in a decent-sized saucepan and cover with just enough water so they're submerged. Add the salt, then place the pan over a cranking heat, pop a lid on and bring to a simmer. Turn the heat down and simmer until they're both soft enough to mash. Drain well and either mash roughly with a fork or the back of a big spoon or, for a smoother result, feed through a potato ricer.

Add the milk and butter to the potatoes and swedes. In the meantime, blanch or fry the kale until cooked to your liking, then stir through the colcannon. Taste for salt and pepper, adding more milk or butter to adjust the consistency (it can vary a lot depending on the potatoes), and serve.

Caramelised Brussels Sprouts with Prosciutto

Serves 6

We make our own prosciutto on the farm, and have done since I moved to the country over a decade ago. Aged for a year, or up to three years, our prosciutto has enjoyed remarkable success, so much so that we don't just eat it raw, we have to find ways to embellish and enhance it. A perfect match, we think, is the darkly caramelised sprout, though they're best frost-sweetened and not long off the bush.

500 g (1 lb 2 oz) brussels sprouts

3–4 tablespoons pork fat

about 12 small, thin slices prosciutto

Trim the base off the sprouts to remove the first couple of leaves. Cut the sprouts in half, through the base.

Heat the pork fat in a heavy-based frying pan over a medium-high heat and fry the sprouts, cut side down, until they are well coloured and starting to soften. Turn them over, and continue cooking to ensure they're cooked in the middle, perhaps getting more colour on the rounded side too, seasoning them a bit in the pan.

Lay the sprouts on a serving plate and lay the prosciutto over, in strips, or perhaps in little bundles. The warmth of the sprouts will bring out all the prosciutto's aroma. A heady, perfect flavour combination, and every bit of it from the farm.

Chargrilled Swedes and Their Leaves

Serves 4 as a side dish

Butter swedes are an incredible thing. I first got mine when the seed company I was buying from just included them with my winter seed purchase, with a note that read, 'We think you've forgotten your swedes! We've included them for you.' I hadn't forgotten to order the seeds, I just didn't know how much I'd love this root vegetable when it's grown with love and cooked fresh. And then I fell in love with them even more when I discovered you could grill them, not just roast or fry or boil or bake. Other varieties of swedes may be more bitter and need a quick blanch before grilling. Butter swede leaves are a pretty awesome veg all on their own, too.

8 butter swedes, scrubbed then halved or quartered, leaves washed and drained

olive oil, for brushing

2 tablespoons butter

1 teaspoon lemon juice

Heat a chargrill pan over a medium heat. Brush the cut sides of the swedes well with the oil, and season with salt and pepper.

Chargrill the swedes over the grill (you can simply roast them if you don't have a grill) until well coloured and tender. Test by inserting a little knife into the swedes. It shouldn't meet any resistance. If the swedes are getting too dark on the grill but aren't tender, finish in a low (150°C/300°F) oven.

Heat the butter in a frying pan over a moderate to high heat and quickly toss the leaves to wilt. Add the lemon juice, turn off, and serve the chargrilled swedes with their leaves over, topped with any pan juices from the leaves.

Daikon, Fennel and Kohlrabi Slaw with Pickled Nasturtium Seeds

Serves 6

This crunchy, palate-cleansing salad has the heat of a bit of daikon, the anise of fennel, and the warm sweetness of kohlrabi. It makes a nice break from the heaviness of winter vegetables, and can be used to match rich meats, such as goulash (see page 272) or brisket (see page 73), or the like. Pickled nasturtium seeds are something we make on the farm, but you can use capers instead.

1 small purple daikon, scrubbed and finely sliced

1 medium fennel head, root removed, cleaned and finely sliced

1 large kohlrabi head, peeled and cut into fine slivers

juice of 1 lemon

3–4 tablespoons extra-virgin olive oil

2–3 teaspoons Pickled Nasturtium Seeds (see Note), drained and rinsed then sliced, or use capers that have been drained and rinsed

Toss the vegetables in a large bowl with the lemon juice, olive oil and some salt and pepper to taste. Mix in the nasturtium seeds, and serve in a salad bowl or similar.

Note

To pickle nasturtium seeds, place 200 g (7 oz) nasturtium seeds in a small, non reactive dish, jar or bowl. Heat 200 ml (7 fl oz) water with 10 g (¼ oz) fine salt just enough to dissolve the salt, then pour over the seeds. Allow to stand at room temperature for 24 hours, covered with a loose fitting lid or cloth. Drain and discard the liquid. Place in a heatproof bowl, boil 250 ml (8½ fl oz) cider vinegar with 5 g salt and ½ teaspoon sugar, and when just simmering, pour over the nasturtiums. Allow to stand for 10 minutes, transfer to a sterile jar (see Note on page 192), pop on a lid, and refrigerate. Allow to pickle for a month before using. Let your taste be the guide. They get better with time. Often the seeds are big, and are best cut or crushed prior to using.

Roasted Parsnip and Chickpea Soup

Serves 8

The luscious sweetness of parsnips mixed with the nuttiness of chickpeas makes for a pretty damn fine warming soup. We find this a fantastic way to use up any leftover roasted parsnips, but fresh parsnips work really well too. Sometimes I use leftover roasted carrots in the mix if I have them, and if the sage is struggling with the winter temperatures, substitute with a bit of rosemary instead.

200 g (7 oz) chickpeas, soaked overnight if possible

1 onion, peeled

2 bay leaves

2–3 tablespoons olive oil

1 leek, white part only, diced

1 sage sprig, plus extra chopped fresh sage to garnish

8 roasted parsnips, diced

2 tablespoons extra-virgin olive oil

crusty bread, to serve

Pop the chickpeas into a large saucepan with the whole onion, bay leaves and 2 litres (68 fl oz/8 cups) water. Bring to a simmer over a high heat, then turn down the heat and cook for about 1 hour.

In another pan, heat the oil and fry the leek over a low heat for about 5 minutes to soften and perhaps just start to colour ever so slightly. Add the sprig of sage, the chickpeas (with their cooking water) and the parsnip. Discard the onion at this stage. Simmer gently for another 30 minutes, or until the chickpeas are buttery soft. Keep an eye on the water level – it should always be about 1 cm (½ in) above the chickpeas.

When the chickpeas are cooked, discard the bay leaves and sage sprig. Take out about one-quarter of the mixture and pulse it in a food processor or whiz with a hand-held blender. (You could even just pulse the whole soup with a hand-held blender; the idea is to add some body to the soup but keep it chunky at the same time, so don't overdo it.) Add this back to the soup. Season to taste. Simmer for another 5 minutes, adding the extra sage right at the end.

Serve in suitably deep bowls drizzled with extra-virgin olive oil, some crusty bread and a decent red.

Potatoes – Varieties and Uses

I didn't really get potatoes until I moved to Tassie. Yes, I did grow up near a market in Canberra where there were more than just the three types (washed, dirty, and chats – baby spuds), but I never understood potato flavour until I moved here.

That's because Tasmanians grow great spuds. And the locals all have a favoured patch, a favoured variety. The ones you buy in shops are usually quite old. When the skins set, they keep for ages in cold storage, and that's a great thing to do with the harvest. But the best potatoes are harvested young. We call it 'bandicooting', where we mimic the local marsupial and create bandicoot holes around the soil at the top of the plant to harvest the sweet, young potatoes that ring the stem. These potatoes, garnered before the tops die down, are the duck's guts of spuds.

If you grow potatoes, the sweetest potatoes – with a skin that comes off with a harsh sideways glance – are the ones from a plant where the top hasn't died off yet. These, you store in the fridge. Let the tops die down completely, then the skins will have set, making for a starchier, but longer-lasting spud. Once they're dry, potatoes with a set skin can be stored in cellar-like conditions: cool, dark and relatively dry.

Tassie potatoes are usually the best part of any meal. Here's what we think of a few varieties.

Pink Eyes

A waxy, sweet-flavoured truly Tasmanian variety of potato that's good for salads or simply boiled. Best pulled fresh from the earth before their skin sets, quickly rinsed under the tap, boiled and tossed with butter.

Dutch Creams and Nicolas

We harvest these as the pink eyes are getting too fat to be called new potatoes. They are our favourite waxy potato: great boiled, mashed or roasted.

King Edwards

We leave these in the ground until the green tops have died back completely. As the skin sets, the sugars convert to starch. This is the perfect floury potato, perfect for steaming and mashing, for baking whole, or if you're in the mood, douse them in beef fat and bung them in the oven for a fluffy tasty roast spud.

Coliban

The perfect potato to sell rather than eat. This is the usual 'washed' variety you'll find in supermarkets because they look pale and handsome. The skin usually separates off, including some flesh, when cooked. Starchy, these are a bit of a rubbish spud for all except those selling them. As Monty Python would say, a potato for laying down and avoiding.

Kipfler

You need a good vegetable brush to get the dirt out of the nooks and crannies of these long, crooked, finger-like potatoes, but worth the effort for a great potato salad. Waxy and sweet, they hold up really well boiled.

Pink Fir Apple

We've never had much luck growing pink fir apples. We can grow them but they're floury. Probably something to do with our soil. If you can get a hold of good ones from a farmers' market, they are a beautiful, dense, waxy salad potato. Great for chunky vegetable soups and braises as they don't fall apart.

What works for us doesn't always work in other climates and soils. Get to know your local potato grower and what she (and her soil) are good at growing.

Jerusalem Artichokes with Lemony Bread Sauce

Serves 6

These incredible-flavoured knobbly tubers are not real artichokes, but are just as delicious. They have a sweet flavour backed with primal earthy notes that are almost truffle-like at times. Here, they get a bit of garlicky richness from a form of bread sauce, with inspiration from a wonderfully talented chef who came and worked with us for a year, Mike Layfield.

500 g (1 lb 2 oz) Jerusalem artichokes, scrubbed well and cut into even-sized chunks

olive oil, for roasting and searing

100 ml (3½ fl oz) Bread Sauce (page 300, the lemon adaptation)

10 small kale leaves, tough ribs removed

Preheat the oven to 220°C (430°F).

Toss the artichokes in a roasting tin with enough oil to just coat, and season well with salt and pepper. Roast for about 40 minutes, tossing regularly so the artichokes don't stick to the tin and colour up nicely. They can stick readily, so don't panic, just add a touch of water to the hot pan – only a tablespoon or two at first – and gently try to scrape them from the base; you want all that sticky, caramelised goodness.

To serve, warm the bread sauce just gently. Blanch the kale leaves in boiling water for a few minutes, then drain well and sear in a hot pan with a little olive oil. Put the bread sauce on a platter or plate, add the artichokes on top and garnish with the kale.

Buttered Salsify with Coppa

Serves 8 as an appetiser

Salsify, a member of the sunflower family, is a lovely root vegetable that is in some of Australia's oldest cookbooks. It's seen a resurgence lately, because it's so damn nice to eat. The best is the scorzonera, the black-skinned variety, and it's delicious to eat just buttered. Here, we've added a little cured meat to make it a nice pre-dinner snack.

8 salsify roots

20 g (¾ oz) butter

8 thin slices coppa, or try prosciutto

Wash the salsify, then peel. Place in the base of a saucepan with 125 ml (4 fl oz/½ cup) water and the butter. Season with a bit of salt and pepper, then poach over a medium heat for about 10 minutes, or until softened well, turning often. You want some residual bite. Drain a little, then wrap each one in the coppa and serve.

Polish Salami with Kohlrabi Remoulade

Serves 6

Kohlrabi is this alien-looking vegetable, often purple-rinded, that grows just above the ground. It is terrific raw, cut into batons, and has a sweet, broccoli-like character, but with more complexity and less of a chlorophyll flavour. It's the perfect foil, enriched with a mayonnaise dressing, for good salami. Usual remoulade has anchovy in it, but that flavour doesn't really go well with the cured pork in this instance.

100 g (3½ oz) Mayonnaise (page 300)

1 tablespoon chopped flat-leaf (Italian) parsley

1 tablespoon chopped chervil (if you have it), or use tarragon

1 teaspoon French-style mustard

2 teaspoons snipped chives (or a tiny bit of red onion)

1 tablespoon chopped capers

2 tablespoons chopped gherkin (pickles)

1 kohlrabi head, peeled and sliced into thin batons

200 g (7 oz) Polish salami, finely sliced

Combine all the ingredients, except the kohlrabi and salami, in a bowl. Add the kohlrabi, mix well and season to taste with salt and pepper. This is often better if made an hour before serving.

When you're ready to eat, lay the salami out on a platter, then lay the kohlrabi mix over the top. Serve immediately.

Pancetta and Cavolo Nero Risotto

Serves 4–5

My risotto changes with the seasons, depending on what's around in the larder and the fridge. In the cooler months, I often try to use cabbage or kale, or cavolo nero, which is a type of kale often called black or Tuscan kale. An extra bit of cured meat in with it can negate the need for stock. You could also use a good pecorino in this if you can get it.

30 g (1 oz) butter

150 g (5½ oz) pancetta, finely diced

2 medium onions, peeled and finely diced

400 g (14 oz) Italian risotto rice (vialone nano is the most idiot-proof, but arborio works okay, too)

375 ml (12½ fl oz/1½ cups) white wine

good handful of cavolo nero (Tuscan kale), hard central ribs removed, leaves finely shredded

2 litres (68 fl oz/8 cup) home-made chicken stock, simmering (or use water rather than bought stock)

80 g (2¾ oz) cooked curd-style cheese, such as piave or gruyère, finely grated

Heat the butter in a large saucepan and gently fry the pancetta to release some of its fat. Add the onion and cook over a medium heat for 5 minutes, stirring occasionally so that it doesn't brown. Continue this gentle frying, with a lid on, until the onion is soft.

Increase the heat and stir in the rice. Fry until it's warm, stirring the whole time. Test this by squeezing a grain between your fingers – the warmth should come through from the centre. Slosh in the wine, throw in the cavolo nero and stir constantly as the wine evaporates. Turn the heat down to medium so the rice continues to boil. When the rice has absorbed just about all the wine, start adding the stock, one ladle at a time, stirring constantly as you do so and waiting until the stock has been absorbed between each addition.

Continue to add the stock, stirring for about 15–20 minutes, then check the rice. You want it to be firm, but not grainy. When it's ready, stir in half of the cheese. Taste for salt and pepper. For some reason, risotto gets better if left to sit for 5 minutes before serving.

Spoon onto a plate and serve with the remaining cheese on the table. It'd be good to have a salad on the side, too.

Broccoli Shoots with Curd and Hazelnuts

Serves 6

The thing about broccoli, when you grow it, is that it is more giving than cauliflower. They both go in the ground at the same time and take up the same amount of space per plant. They're both winter vegetables, predominantly, in our part of the world. But a cauliflower just gives you one head per plant, whereas broccoli, after the first big head, will give you lovely shoots. These go from winter and, with some varieties, right into spring. Unlike broccolini, which is a hybrid and has intellectual rights attached to it, you don't have to pay royalties for the use of it. Look for the delicious shoots at farmers' markets.

500 g (1 lb 2 oz) broccoli heads

2–3 tablespoons extra-virgin olive oil

juice of ½ lemon

80 g (2¾ oz) goat's curd, or similar

50 g (1¾ oz) roasted hazelnuts, or other nuts, lightly crushed

Put the broccoli in a saucepan with about 1 cm (½ in) of boiling water and cover with a lid. Place over a very high flame and cook for about 3–4 minutes to quickly steam the broccoli. Drain well. Toss with the olive oil, some salt and pepper and the lemon juice to taste.

Spread the curd on a plate, top with the broccoli and hail the nuts down over the top. Serve hot.

L'abbacchio (Wood Oven–roasted Lamb Leg in the Roman Style)

Serves 5–6

L'abbacchio is a Roman dish of roasted lamb that's traditionally cooked in chunks. Here's a version using a whole leg. I tend to cook it less than the Romans do, but that's more to do with the quality of lamb I can get (and personal preference) than anything else. You can add a mashed anchovy fillet with the vinegar, but I tend to leave it out.

2 tablespoons olive oil (or, even better, lard)

3 long slices prosciutto, cut into strips

1.5 kg (3 lb 5 oz) lamb leg, scored in deep cuts about 5 cm (2 in) apart

10 garlic cloves

1 rosemary sprig

15 sage leaves

2 tablespoons wine vinegar, either colour

Preheat the oven to 170°C (340°F).

In a large, ovenproof pot, heat the oil and fry the prosciutto just until the fat starts to melt. Add the lamb and brown the outside well. Drain off the fat. Season with salt and pepper, then add the garlic, rosemary and sage and cover with a lid.

Transfer to the oven and cook for about 40 minutes. Take the lid off, add the vinegar, toss to combine and cook for another 5–10 minutes or so without the lid.

It's traditionally served with roasted potatoes (see page 298), and I'd have a big dish of wilted kale on the side too.

Beef Cheek Pie

Serves 6 generously

The more a muscle works, the more flavour it has, and a cow chews a lot. So the cheek is packed full of beefy flavour. Here, I've matched that intensity with a hint of Worcestershire and mustard for a lovely, chunky pie.

1–2 tablespoons lard, dripping or butter

2 large onions, peeled and diced

1 kg (2 lb 3 oz) beef cheeks

2–3 tablespoons plain (all-purpose) flour

80 g (2¾ oz/⅓ cup) tomato passata (puréed tomatoes)

250 ml (8½ fl oz/1 cup) dry red wine

750 ml (25½ fl oz/3 cups) water or beef stock

3 tablespoons Worcestershire sauce

3 teaspoons French-style mustard, plus extra to serve

2 bay leaves

1 quantity Lard Yoghurt Pastry (page 301)

1 free-range egg, beaten with a splash of water

tomato sauce (ketchup), to serve

Heat the lard in a large saucepan over a medium flame. Fry the onion until well softened and starting to brown. Remove with a slotted spoon and keep to one side.

Dust the beef with the flour and fry in the lard to brown on all sides. Do it in batches so the meat doesn't stew, rubbing the yummy stuck-on bits from the bottom of the pan as you go. Set aside the meat with the onions. In the same pan, fry the tomato passata, stirring constantly, until it starts to colour, then tip in the wine and boil vigorously while scraping the base of the pan with a wooden spoon to loosen the stuck-on flour.

Return the onions and meat to the pan with the water, Worcestershire, mustard and bay leaves. Bring to the boil, then turn the heat right down and simmer, stirring often, for about 1½ hours, or until the meat is tender. If the sauce is getting gluggy, add a tablespoon or two more water as it cooks, or put a lid on.

Remove the cheeks, cut them into chunks to suit your pie, then return them to the sauce. It's best if this mix isn't too hot when you fill the pie, but don't stress about it.

Preheat the oven to 190°C (375°F).

Take two-thirds of the pastry and divide into six even-sized balls. Roll each ball out to fit 8 cm (3¼ in) wide by 8 cm (3¼ in) deep individual pie dishes, or similar. Fill with the meat mixture, which should now be coated in a rich, thick sauce. Roll out the remaining pastry and cut out discs to cover the tops of the pies. Crimp the edges together and cut a slit in the top to let the steam escape.

Brush the top with the egg wash. Bake towards the bottom of the oven for about 30–40 minutes, or until the pastry is deep brown. Serve hot with lots of tomato sauce and mustard.

Beef Brisket with Mustard and Beer

Serves 4

Brisket, the bony, fatty cut from the top of the chest of a cow, is the best-flavoured piece of meat. But it does take a long time to cook, and the meat can be hidden between ribs, or under fat. The intense, delightful flavour makes it worth every bit of effort.

2 large onions, peeled

2 kg (4 lb 6 oz) brisket, on the bone

2–3 tablespoons French-style mustard

125 ml (4 fl oz/½ cup) amber ale

Preheat the oven to 150°C (300°F).

Cut the onions crossways into rounds about 1 cm (½ in) thick. Place in the bottom of a deep roasting tin. Rub the brisket well all over with the mustard and place it in the tray on top of the onion. Season the meat well with salt, then pour the beer into the tray along with about 1 litre (34 fl oz/4 cups) water. Cover the meat with some baking paper (to help hold in the steam and juices), then cover the tray well with foil or a tight-fitting lid.

Bake the meat for at least 4 hours, or until it is so soft it is falling from the bone, then remove from the oven and set aside. Drain the juices into a jug and refrigerate to set the fat. With the meat, now's the time to get your hands dirty; there's really no other way to do it successfully. When the meat is cool enough to handle, strip all the meat you can find from around the bones and discard the bones and fat.

When the fat has set on top of the juices, preheat the oven to 180°C (350°F). Remove the fat and reserve for other uses (such as the Caramelised Beef Fat Roasted Turnips on page 75), then mix the cooking juices back in with the meat in an ovenproof dish.

Cook the meat in the oven for 30 minutes or so, to cook the juices back into the meat and give the meat some colour. Taste for seasoning. This glorious dark, rich, heady flavoured brisket can be served with roasted swedes or colcannon (mash with cabbage or kale mixed through it, see page 51), or other root vegetables, such as turnips, but it does need something light to accompany it, like a salad or steamed carrots, to cut the richness.

Goat Pie with Lard Yoghurt Pastry

Serves 6

We got some goats, and the deal was that if they ate the blackberries, we wouldn't eat them. And, so far, they've held up their part of the deal, even if they didn't know there was a deal. But in the meantime, we've been eating a bit of goat meat from someone else's farm, and it's particularly grand in a pie.

4–5 tablespoons olive oil

2 large onions, peeled and diced

4 carrots, scrubbed and diced

2 celery stalks, cleaned and diced

1 kg (2 lb 3 oz) goat shoulder, diced

50 g (1¾ oz/⅓ cup) plain (all-purpose) flour

80 g (2¾ oz/⅓ cup) tomato passata (puréed tomatoes)

1 teaspoon ground cinnamon

1 teaspoon ground allspice

2 bay leaves

1 tablespoon rosemary leaves

1 quantity Lard Yoghurt Pastry (page 301)

1 free-range egg, beaten with a splash of water (optional)

Heat 2 tablespoons of the oil in a large, heavy-based saucepan over a medium heat. Fry the onion, carrots and celery well, for about 10 minutes, to really soften. Remove with a slotted spoon and keep the veg to one side.

Toss the goat with the flour to coat it lightly. Heat the same saucepan over a medium-high flame, add another 2 tablespoons oil and fry the meat well to brown all over, adding a touch more oil if necessary and rubbing a wooden spatula over the base of the pan to stop the flour sticking and scorching. When the meat is brown, add the tomato and cook, stirring constantly, for 1 minute. Return the vegetables to the pan, throw in the spices and herbs, and add enough water to cover the meat, about 1 litre (34 fl oz/ 4 cups). Stir well as it comes to the boil, then turn down and simmer for about 1½ hours, or until the goat is tender. Stir it often during this time, to stop it sticking, and add more water if it's getting too thick or the meat isn't covered anymore.

When the meat is tender, remove the pan from the heat and allow to cool.

Preheat the oven to 180°C (350°F).

In the meantime, make the pastry. When ready to assemble, divide the pastry into six even parts. Take two-thirds of each piece and roll into balls. Then, on a well-floured board, roll each ball out to fit a 10 cm (4 in) individual pie dish or similar.

Line the six pie dishes with this pastry, fill with the goat meat, pressing down to remove any air pockets and leaving enough space to attach the lid. Roll the rest of the pastry ball on a well-floured board to form the lids. Lay the lids on top of each pie and pinch the pastry together at the edges to seal. Cut a small incision in the top to release the steam. You can brush the tops with a little egg wash to make a glossier, more golden finished pie, too.

Bake in the centre of the oven for about 30–40 minutes, or until golden.

Roasted Sausages, Olives and Bay

Serves 4–6

This is a rustic, delicious dish of bangers simply cooked in the oven in a rich, oniony sauce. The best sausages to use are pure pork ones with no starch added, and coarsely ground in the southern French or Italian style.

2–3 tablespoons olive oil

4 medium onions, peeled and finely sliced

4 bay leaves, fresh if possible

4–5 fresh thyme sprigs

1 anchovy, crushed or chopped

50 g (1¾ oz) black olives

1 kg (2 lb 3 oz) pork and fennel sausages, or similar

crusty bread, roasted spuds or polenta, to serve

Heat the oil in a large, preferably heavy-based frying pan over a medium heat and fry the onions, bay leaves and thyme, stirring regularly, until the onions soften well. (This could take about 30 minutes, so be patient.)

Preheat the oven to 180°C (350°F).

Add the anchovy and cook for about another 5 minutes. Stir in the black olives and transfer the onion mix to an ovenproof dish or frying pan. Nestle the sausages amongst the onion and bake for about 10 minutes, or until the sausages start to colour. Turn them over and bake for another 8–10 minutes so they colour on the other side.

Serve hot, with bread, spuds, or even polenta.

Caramelised Beef Fat Roasted Turnips

Serves 8 as a side dish

Turnips – the European variety – have a hardy, mouth-watering bitterness that some love and some find confronting. I really like to contrast that bitterness with some caramelising of the natural sugars in the veg, and beef fat is the natural companion. Vegetarians can give olive oil a go, too.

1 kg (2 lb 3 oz) turnips, scrubbed and quartered

1 teaspoon salt, plus extra to serve

3–4 tablespoons beef fat, or more (pork fat also works a treat)

Preheat the oven to 220°C (430°F).

Place the turnips in a saucepan, cover with water, add the salt, then pop on a lid and place the pan over a very high heat. Bring to the boil, then drain immediately. With the lid on the pan, shake the turnips vigorously to soften the surface slightly.

Heat an ovenproof frying pan over a very high heat until hot, then add the beef fat and slide the turnips in, allowing them to dry a little more (there's always some moisture on the outside after simmering). Use a spatula or similar to turn them and coat them with the oil. Transfer the pan to the oven and roast the turnips until they are well browned – dark brown but not black – on the cut surfaces. Drain on paper towel, season with salt, and serve hot.

Australia's first ever commercial saffron crop was grown just near our front gate. Ninety per cent rotted into the ground, however, because of our wet soil. Terry and Nicky Noonan, the growers, didn't give up and, two decades later, it's still grown on our road, just a bit further up the hill where it's drier.

Saffron Rice Pudding

Serves 4–6

I grew up with rice pudding: a filling, nutritious, sweet treat that filled the house with great smells and filled our bellies when we were still hungry post dinner. Dad always got the fly's walk, the wonderful skin on the top, when I was growing up. Now I'm bigger, I get that too. Here, it's poshed up with some incredible Tasmanian saffron.

625 ml (21 fl oz/2½ cups) full-cream (whole) milk

125 ml (4 fl oz/½ cup) pouring (single/light) cream

finely grated zest of ½ orange (or, even better, a little kumquat)

generous pinch of saffron threads, ideally soaked in 1 tablespoon milk for 24 hours

3 green cardamom pods

110 g (4 oz/½ cup) raw (demerara) sugar

75 g (2¾ oz/⅓ cup) short-grain rice

a few drops of vanilla extract

Preheat the oven to low, about 140–150°C (275–300°F).

Place the milk, cream, orange zest, saffron and cardamom in a large saucepan and bring to a simmer. Turn off the heat and let it stand for 15 minutes to allow the flavours to combine. It should be fragrant already, and starting to leach colour from the saffron. Pour into a 1.5 litre (51 fl oz/6 cup) casserole dish with the sugar, rice and vanilla.

Cook in the oven for 1½ hours, or until completely cooked, stirring after about 30 minutes, and then allowing it to form a nice brown skin towards the end. The pudding may be a little runny, with the rice grains plump yet still retaining their integrity. The nice thing is that it thickens gently a bit as it sits, so waiting 30 minutes or so before eating it isn't a bad thing. Serve warm.

Parkin

Makes about 40 squares

Parkin is a lovely, sticky, gingery cake-slice thing, traditionally eaten on Guy Fawkes Night (5th November) in the UK, hence its presence during our firelit colder winter days. It gets better after a few days.

450 g (1 lb) golden syrup

225 g (8 oz) treacle

2 tablespoons milk

100 g (3½ oz) butter, plus extra for greasing

100 g (3½ oz) lard

450 g (1 lb) fine oatmeal (use quick-cooking oats at a pinch)

200 g (7 oz/1⅓ cups) plain (all-purpose) flour

2 teaspoons bicarbonate of soda (baking soda)

2 teaspoons ground ginger

1 teaspoon mixed spice

pinch of salt

2 large free-range eggs, beaten lightly

Preheat the oven to 130°C (265°F). Grease and line a 30 × 30 cm (12 × 12 in) slice tin, or similar.

Combine the golden syrup, treacle, milk, butter and lard in a saucepan and warm over a low heat just until it's all soft and melted. Don't boil it though.

In a large bowl, mix the oatmeal, flour, bicarb, ginger, mixed spice and salt and pour in the warm syrup mix. Stir well, then add the eggs and pour into the prepared tin.

Bake for about 1½ hours, or until the batter has set into a nice, sticky slice. Cut the parkin into 3 cm (1¼ in) squares and, ideally, leave for a few days before eating.

Chocolate Éclairs

Makes about 30 small éclairs

It's really important to beat the eggs into the dough well. Use a machine if you have one. You'll need to use the 'k', sometimes known as 'bishop's hat' beater for the best effect. That's the one that's not a dough hook and not a whisk.

130 g (4½ oz) butter

150 g (5½ oz) plain (all-purpose) flour

2 teaspoons caster (superfine) sugar

4 free-range eggs

1 quantity Pastry Cream (page 312)

Chocolate Topping

100 g (3½ oz) dark chocolate, broken into small bits

40 g (1½ oz) butter

Preheat the oven to 225°C (435°F) and line two baking trays.

Combine the butter with 300 ml (10 fl oz) water in a saucepan and heat gently. When the butter has melted, bring the mixture to the boil and, as it boils, throw all the flour and sugar into the pan at once and beat rapidly with a wooden spoon. Keep the pan on a low heat and continue beating until the dough forms a smooth ball and comes away from the edge of the pan. It's important to cook this dough enough, but not brown it.

Remove from the heat and allow to cool for a couple of minutes, then beat in the eggs really well, one at a time.

This mixture is then ready for piping into logs or balls on the prepared trays. Keep them small and delicate, as they will often more than double in volume while cooking.

Bake for 15 minutes, then reduce the heat to 180°C (350°F) and cook until golden brown and firm. You can cool them in the switched-off oven (with the door ajar) if you like, to crisp them even more. Some cooks even pierce the ends with a skewer while the pastry is fresh from the oven, to let out steam, and continue to bake them at a lower heat to dry them out. Cool well on wire racks.

For the chocolate topping, place the chocolate and butter in a small, heatproof bowl and melt over a saucepan of just simmering water, stirring often until melted.

To assemble, fill a piping (icing) bag with the pastry cream. Cut the éclairs in half lengthways, then dip the top pieces in the chocolate. Allow to set for a few minutes, then pipe the pastry cream into each one. Serve immediately or within an hour or two for best results.

Olga's Cake

Serves 10

Olga is a friend of my mum's, and this is her cake. It's one of those lovely European poppy seed cakes, moistened with apples.

- butter, for greasing
- 7 free-range eggs, separated
- 190 g (6½ oz) caster (superfine) sugar
- 250 g (9 oz) poppy seeds
- 180 ml (6 fl oz) vegetable oil
- 2 tablespoons self-raising flour
- 1 large, green cooking apple (approx. 200 g/7 oz), coarsely grated with the skin on
- icing (confectioner's) sugar, for dusting

Preheat the oven to 180°C (350°F). Grease and line a deep 25 cm (10 in) springform cake tin.

Beat the yolks with the sugar until light and pale, either by hand or with an electric mixer. Fold in the poppy seeds, oil, flour and apple.

Using an electric mixer, whisk the egg whites to soft peaks (the point where, when you lift up the beaters, the egg white stays in the little peaks but they bend over at their tips. This means the egg white is still soft and has room to expand).

Fold one-quarter of the egg white into the poppy seed mixture, then fold the poppy seed mixture into the remaining egg white.

Pour the mixture into the prepared tin and bake for 1 hour to 1 hour 10 minutes, or until a skewer inserted in the centre of the cake comes out clean.

Dust with icing sugar before serving.

There's no single day when winter breaks. One day, everything just seems to scream spring.

Spring

Apple blossom
Warmth
Long grass
Broad beans
Lambs
Stiff breezes
A surge in bees
A cute calf
Clover
Jersey cream
Birds nesting
Asparagus
Fecundity
Swooping lapwings
More broad beans
Elderflowers
New shoots
Sowing, sowing, sowing
Eggs, at last!

Recipes

It seems like it'll never come. In the midst of a Tassie winter, spring seems too far off. In our little corner of the world, spring seeps into being. The first hints are in early September, but you're never quite sure it'll arrive until late in the month.

You can tell what time someone left the house in spring. Are they wearing an overcoat, a sunhat, a rain jacket or shorts? Spring can be frosty, or even sprinkle a little snow on occasion. But it can also be over 30°C, perhaps even the day after it has snowed. The weather berates us for not wearing enough or too much. It toys with us. The wind awaits our complacency, and the promise of warmth one day can be dashed with an icy blast the next. The cosseting of winter makes way for the unpredictability and excitement of spring. There's the promise of new life as plants surge forth with young growth, and blossoms unfurl and the insect population explodes.

Spring means the chooks are back on the lay, after the recharge of their annual moult. The cows calve. Spring milk is loaded with golden-coloured cream. Goats have their kids in spring, too. New chicks crack open their shells and the cycle of life turns again. Spring lamb is born in spring, named after the season that bore it, not the season you eat it in. We do, however, eat lamb at this time of year, even if it should be called hogget or two tooth: sheep that are over a year old. We like them that way; they've better flavour.

The soil is starting to warm after the long hibernation of winter. Seeds that wouldn't germinate in winter now have a chance to shoot. And while everything grows, there's actually a moment where there's not the usual abundance.

Despite the fecundity, the green, growing gloriousness of this time of year, we call parts of spring, the later parts, 'the hungry patch' because the garden is growing but not yielding. The crops are fattening, but aren't yet ready to harvest. Though perhaps 'hungry patch' is a misnomer. Thanks to 200 asparagus plants, and judicious winter plantings, we never actually go hungry. The variety of crops is, no doubt, lower than the heady days of summer, but there's still variety. If anything, it's more fun in the kitchen, finding new ways with the staples. A turnip pasty, perhaps? Our very own polenta from our stone-ground corn? A spring risotto using whatever is good on the day? Broad beans? (You know you can eat the whole pod if you get them at the right time, and cook them the right way.)

As the season ends, we get strong hints of summer. A ripe strawberry or two. Peas, sugar snaps, the first glimpse of fat gooseberries, though they're still so sour they make your whole body pucker. The elder trees that adorn neighbours' land, however, are fat with umbels, ready for the picking. The umbels are made up of hundreds of tiny blossoms, each one sweetly scented. We scale ladders and fill baskets with elderflowers, as many as we can in the short-but-prolific season, ready to make a delightfully fragrant cordial that will last the summer long.

The Spring

Harvest

September.
Broad bean shoots and leaves, purple-sprouting broccoli, first peas from the greenhouse. Hakurei turnips, daikon and radish, last of the leeks. Eggs.

October.
Green garlic, asparagus, rhubarb. Still heaps of greens. Coriander (cilantro), stinging nettles.

November.
Broad beans, peas, artichokes, potatoes from the frost-free zones. The first flush of strawberries. Rhubarb. The early carrots. Elderflowers.

12
SEPTEMBER

There's a strange warmth. It's nine degrees above average. After months of cold, this warmth, under a cloudless sky, produces a feeling that can't be captured on a thermometer. What's going on? I saw a blowfly already, about two months too early.

One day it's 22°C, the next it's closer to 10°C and forecast to drop below that by the end of the week. This is Tasmania, where the weather swings by and can turn faster than a wallaby on the hop.

On days like this, the chores are not chores. The work always has dignity, even a humble task, but when the sun gifts her warmth without scorching our backs, there's more pleasure attached to the daily routine than it seems right to admit. More joy and fulfilment.

That sun reaches dark places. The asparagus has just started its inexorable journey from the newly warmed soil, each fat finger reaching for the sky before being sliced off by a gardener's knife at ground level. Fresh from the ground, these spears are nutty and incredibly sweet. So different from the bought stuff, especially with a luminescent yellow hollandaise. There are five pea pods that have swelled enough to pick. There's a flush of broccoli shoots, especially the purple ones, fantastic to eat raw, but even better tossed in the wok and served with fresh curd and snappy roasted nuts.

The salami shed is full, the prosciutto hanging for the year. It feels like winter has only just started to release her grip on the land, but the garden is in full flight. The eggplants are germinating in the nursery. So too some of the capsicums and chillies. Beds are cleared of kohlrabi, or beetroot. We will soon say goodbye to the root vegies that have graced our oven trays. Various crops will be eked out until we make it to the hungry patch, still a month away, where broad beans, Asian greens and turnips are king. This year, for the first time, the asparagus will be a welcome addition.

For the first time in months, we've plenty of eggs. The chooks are back on the lay in a serious way. There are duck eggs awaiting incubation, a gift from a stranger. We're resting the cows, so there's no milking for a bit. The two-month break seems like it will pass very quickly – already, I'm halfway through, as the dairy lies dormant. Only six weeks to go until Elsie calves, and then the early morning routine will begin again.

The grass has turned emerald green. The paddocks are starting to become less boggy. A few warm days can do that. It'll be two more months before we can drive right up the property again, though. Three on a bad year. It's one reason we don't have a tractor.

24 SEPTEMBER

The chimney rattles. The wind is relentless as it skims up the valley from the west. Often the rain angles in so far that it looks like it might never make landfall, appearing horizontal as it whips up our valley. What happened to the early warm spell? Fat, heavy raindrops hit the windows on the west high up, sucking warmth from the house, and us, if we're out in it.

On days like this, I try to find something indoors to do. But often our role as caretaker can't be abrogated even for a few hours, and there's no option but to get among it and get wet. I venture out, feeding pigs, making sure the animals are safe, dry and comfortable. If you dress right, you can spend a day getting drenched on the outside and still stay comfy. If you don't dress right, you're probably in the wrong job.

13 OCTOBER

From the farm, looking west, we see wild places. High places far from our almost sea-level address. Today I spy the last of the snow on Adamson's Peak, a reminder of the winter past. Even Sleeping Beauty, the range at the Huon Valley's head that looks like a reclining woman, has shed the dusting of powdery snow on her alpine face.

We've had pockets of frost in the hollows and many days, more than is usual, are warm, and there are even some that are strangely devoid of wind this spring. We feel guilt at the thick, lush green of the grass when the news is full of drought and dust and lack of feed for livestock on the mainland.

I spent the day doing butchery, a task at once daunting and inspiring. The responsibility weighs heavily to ensure we get as much from each pig as we can. I'm not as proficient as those who do it for a living; a good butcher is an artist and generally underrated, but this tactile moment gives me an important connection to the animal that once lived. It's about respect for the life that was given, the food that can, and will, be produced.

I feed the Tassie devils some bones, their screeches in the night a reminder of the wild that once coated all these hills, and the remnants of that wildness that still linger on our borders. These carnivorous marsupials venture near the house on occasion.

We're not sure if it's the devils or the quolls who steal the dog's bones. Tonight, there's enough for everybody.

We've been playing around with the last of the potatoes. There's a lamb and potato pie, scented with saffron grown by our neighbours. There's new bread from the oven, a potato version. In fact, this spring has lots of promise of new things. New calves a few days away. New piglets about to be born to Jackie. And a new farmhand, Rowan, who grew up on a dairy and who talks and walks gently among the animals.

The mud has gone: an El Niño–event forecast. That means dry. We're already watering parts of the garden three times a day, in a month that can swing from frost to 30°C in a couple of days.

We work this soil, walk this farm, with little machinery. We're out in it every day, a part of the environment. We feel the changes under our feet, see it in the coats of the cattle, hear it in the trees. There's talk of how this is the perfect weather for snakes, and suddenly there one is, a fat, metre-long tiger snake warming itself in the sun near the kitchen.

We feel like we live in paradise, and occasionally there are serpents in Eden.

25
OCTOBER

Elsie, our prized Guernsey cow, shuffles her feet. Her tail swishes. For days she's been licking her flanks, as her belly fills to epic proportions. Today, her substantial udder has filled rapidly, as taut as a snare drum, with colostrum – that vital first milk.

Towards dusk, Elsie's waters break. She lies for a bit, then stands. She takes a few minutes' rest on her side as the contractions hit, and first a hoof, then a second hoof and the calf's nose appear. Some enormous effort, and another half an hour, then the head and shoulders of the calf are out. Elsie stands, looks doddery, and lays down again by the time the calf is born. An enthusiastic calf we call Mister, he's up on his feet within 30 minutes, though mum stays prone. Hedley, our nine-year-old son, describes the scene as the 'horrifying beauty of birth' as we head back to the house for a late dinner.

An hour later, and Elsie still hasn't stood. In fact, she's looking weaker, looking bad. Her head is twisted around against her flank. The whites of her eyes are showing. Her snout is dry. Her muscles twitch. Twice before she's had milk fever hours after giving birth. Essentially paralysed, a fat, well-fed cow can go from standing to dead in four hours. Milk fever is treatable, but you have to get onto it early.

When a cow is about to give birth, they produce a lot of milk, and it contains a lot of calcium. Calcium, which we mammals store in bones, is also vital for muscle movement. It's so important for muscles that when our diet is deficient, our bodies have the ability to take calcium from our bones to ensure our brains and muscles continue to work normally.

A well-fed cow who is predisposed to milk fever can lose the ability to rapidly move the mineral efficiently in and out of bones to blood and to muscle. She puts too much into the milk and becomes paralysed. Luckily, the fix is simple. A subcutaneous injection of a fluid that contains calcium can reverse milk fever almost instantly. A bigger cow might need two injections. Elsie is such a cow. We've been down this road with her before.

So, seeing Elsie starting to show some early signs of milk fever, we inject two bags of this magic rejuvenator. It takes a while, but within an hour or two she's sitting normally, her eyes focused, her muscles relaxed. She finishes cleaning her calf, mooing gently at the young bull. We help the calf suckle while she lies, because the earlier he gets his colostrum, the better. Elsie is now far brighter, feistier, more alert. We leave her with food and drink within reach, and go to bed. It's 1 am, and I fall straight to sleep.

It's not only the humans who do the work. We couldn't grow much without bees and other pollinating insects.

26

OCTOBER

I roll out of bed at 3 am and check on Elsie. She's lying in a similar spot. I watch her chew her cud. She's eating and drinking and is still besotted with her calf. Her snout is wet. Her eyes look clear. I stagger back to my still-warm doona.

At 6 am, she's down. A cow down is an awful sight. Instead of lying sternum to the earth, a downer cow will lie unnaturally flat, legs out, flank to earth. A paralysed cow has its legs stiff straight in front, the eyes rolled back in the head so barely any brown is visible, only the bloodshot white. As I race down to where Elsie lies, I can't even see any muscle twitches. I can't see her breathing either, as I use my own lungs at their capacity, yelling up to the farmhouse for help.

I have a deep, deep bond with our milking cows, and none more so than Elsie, who's provided dairy for our table for nearly seven years. So, seeing her motionless, in the death pose, in the steely grey early morning light savages my heart. I think of what we should have done, the hours we should have spent up with her, not trusting that we'd already done our best. We had edged her away from the precipice of death, only to leave her too early, to now find her back there again.

As I kneel and tug at Elsie's head, the eye moves slightly. She takes a shallow breath. There's life in her yet. With Sadie's help, dressed in her dressing gown and still addled by sleep, we inject Elsie with more calcium. We lift her impossibly heavy head to help expel gas she might've trapped in her fermenting stomach. We find thick woolly blankets to warm her body, packing her with hay all around. If we had a god that we believed in, we'd pray.

And, little by little, life returns. The breathing deepens. Elsie's eye, the one facing me and the sky, stops rolling. Eventually, her legs soften enough to bend at the joins, meaning that some of the paralysis has passed. She doesn't sit up. Still she lies, shivering, in a way that is so unnatural for a cow that all her organs are in the wrong spot, her stomachs compressed, her breathing difficult.

But, most importantly, Elsie lives.

Eventually, with farmhand Rowan's help, I get her to stand: a wobbly, inelegant-looking shadow of her former self. But stand she does. When we've got her up after episodes of milk fever in previous years, we've felt a little like saviours – that we have fulfilled our role as guardians. Today, knowing Elsie's history, knowing how quickly the illness can strike, and knowing we had still managed to let her get to death's door within metres of the house, today we only feel guilty.

I think most farmers would be familiar with the sense of responsibility we feel for our livestock. I don't think Sadie and I are unusual amongst those who live on the land. Most farmers put themselves in harm's way, sacrifice a lot of their lives, and take on a large emotional burden, to care for animals. That may seem counter-intuitive to those not at the coalface. It may seem strange that those who will one day decide an animal will die are also those who care most for it while it lives. But wanting a low-stress, healthy life for their animals is the remit of good farmers.

4 NOVEMBER

Elsie has bounced back, though her age is starting to show, and we know this will be a short and last milking. We'll retire her on the farm in the coming months.

The season is in full glory. Our garden keeps bursting forth, all the fruit trees cloaked in leaves, belying a time of less variety from the land. Those sweet, crunchy hakurei turnips, which help fill the gap, are magnificent with dried fennel fronds and lemon.

We pod peas, eat peas, serve peas. A flush of sweet green pods is the signal that warm weather has set in. They remind me again that ours isn't a restaurant in the normal sense, that what we do is a bit different, by definition. We are trying to serve the best home-cooked food a restaurant can produce. Because peas turn most of their sugars to starch in the first few hours after picking, and because freshly grown asparagus changes from the moment it is plucked from the soil, we are lucky enough to be able to serve them at their absolute peak. Our purpose, at home and our eatery, is one of capturing flavour: the flavour of properly grown, properly cooked food that you can only really get if you cook at home, if you are close to the producer, to the earth. Restaurants have to pre-cook, to pre-harvest, to make do with things two days, three days, three weeks out of the ground. Rarely does produce improve with age. A fridge isn't a hospital, and most things don't get better in there.

Only by having a garden on site, like so many do at home, can you reap the absolute best flavour from your greens. Everything else is a hollow confection.

Asparagus Frittata

Serves 1

A real frittata isn't a quiche without pastry; it's an omelette. Here, asparagus, that spring favourite, comes to the fore. You need good eggs and good cheese in this to make it really taste great.

3 free-range eggs

1 tablespoon grated parmesan

2 teaspoons extra-virgin olive oil

3–4 fat asparagus spears, cut thinly on an angle

fresh chopped herbs, to garnish (optional)

Use a fork to whisk the eggs with the parmesan and some salt and pepper. (Using a fork seems to give a fluffier end result, meaning a lighter feel in the mouth.) Stir in 2 teaspoons water.

Preheat the grill (broiler) to high.

Heat the oil in a frying pan over a moderately high heat and fry the asparagus for just 1 minute or so, tossing every now and then, or until it has cooked through. Stir in the eggs, rubbing the bottom of the pan with the back of a fork so the mixture doesn't burn, just as you would an omelette. You could even add a little fresh parsley, some tarragon, or a little fresh thyme to the mix here to enliven it, but the pure asparagus flavour is pretty damn fine on its own.

When it's nearly set, place the pan under the grill to set the top. Serve straight away, perhaps with some fresh herbs to garnish.

Asparagus and Shiitake Flan

Serves 6

While we sometimes get our own mushrooms from the inoculated logs we have on the farm, we're also lucky enough to have a local shiitake grower at Cygnet, and the flavour, especially when paired with our own asparagus, is extraordinary.

1 quantity Lard Shortcrust Pastry (page 301)

4 free-range eggs

250 g (9 oz/1 cup) sour cream

2 bay leaves, ideally fresh

15 fresh shiitakes, destalked (the stalks are good for stocks), or use other medium-sized mushrooms

2–3 asparagus spears, tough ends removed, stems cut into 2–3 cm (¾–1¼ in) pieces on an angle

6 whole roasted garlic cloves, peeled

generous pinch or two of grated nutmeg

leaves from 2–3 fresh thyme sprigs

40 g (1½ oz/⅓ cup) grated cheddar, or similar (try parmesan or gruyère)

Roll out the pastry to fit a 30 × 20 × 2 cm (12 × 8 × ¾ in) tray or flan dish. Refrigerate for 30 minutes.

Preheat the oven to 180°C (350°F).

Blind-bake the pastry (see Note below). Once baked, leave the pastry to rest while you whisk the eggs then whisk in the sour cream. Add the bay leaves and steep for about 30 minutes, then season to taste with salt and pepper.

Reheat the oven to 180°C (350°F).

Lay the shiitake caps out evenly over the pastry base, slicing them if they're large. Dot the asparagus and garlic around too. Whisk some of the nutmeg into the sour cream mixture and carefully pour this mixture between the shiitakes (it's probably best to leave the bay leaves in the bowl, or just fish them out). Don't overfill the pastry case or the custard will run over the side and make it very hard to remove the flan from the tin. Add a touch more nutmeg, sprinkle over the thyme leaves and the cheese. Bake for 15–20 minutes, or until the mixture is set and ideally a little bit brown. Serve warm, or at room temperature.

Note on Blind-baking

Roll out the pastry to fit your tin. Refrigerate well (or even freeze for 30 minutes). Preheat the oven to 180°C (350°F), then line the pastry with non-stick paper and weigh down with uncooked beans or rice or similar. Metal works really well because it conducts heat through from the top, so a big pile of sixpences would be nice, but most people use pulses or rice and re-use. The weight stops the pastry from puffing in the middle as it bakes, but it does slow the cooking of the base down. Bake for about 10–15 minutes, or until the pastry is starting to colour and cook through. Remove the paper and beans and bake for another 5–10 minutes at about 160°C (315°F) to crisp up the base. It's often a good idea to protect the edges with foil in the last baking to avoid them browning too much while the base cooks.

Soft Polenta with Green Garlic

Serves at least 6

We grow a variety of flint corn: a starchy corn that isn't a true polenta variety, but oh my, does it make a cracking polenta. The glorious yellow, orange, purple and white of the various kernels mix to a less-attractive browny grey, but what it lacks in bold colour, it makes up for in flavour.

2 teaspoons salt

350 g (12½ oz/2⅓ cups) polenta

50 g (1¾ oz) butter, plus 100 g (3½ oz) extra

2 stalks green garlic, cleaned and chopped

100 g (3½ oz/1 cup) parmesan, grated

Heat 2 litres (68 fl oz/8 cups) water in a large saucepan over a robust flame until nearly boiling, then add the salt and sprinkle in the polenta, stirring constantly. Maybe even whisk it at this point to make sure no lumps form; you really don't want lumps.

Bring to the boil, then reduce the heat and simmer very gently for at least 40 minutes, stirring constantly with a flat-bottomed spatula to stop the polenta from sticking. (You can pause at times, as I've done, and the polenta still ends up yummy.) If it becomes too hard to stir as it thickens, add a little more water, particularly in the last 10 minutes, but don't add too much or the flavour will end up watery too.

Heat the butter in a frying pan over a low heat and fry the garlic just enough to soften it.

Stir the extra butter and cheese into the polenta until melted and taste for seasoning. Serve immediately with the green garlic, or possibly a meat-based ragu.

Spring Garlic and Spinach Tart

Serves 4

We grow a lot of our own garlic, but there's a window of time where the stuff in the ground doesn't have big fat bulbs yet and the garlic from last year has all sprouted. It's at this magic moment that we use spring garlic: the straight, leek-looking stems of growing garlic. It's milder and sweeter, and lovely in a tart like this. Clean it as you would a leek, discarding any really tough green bits and watching for dirt between the leaves.

salad, to serve

Pastry

150 g (5½ oz) butter, chilled and diced

300 g (10½ oz/2 cups) plain (all-purpose) flour

good pinch of salt

2 tablespoons plain yoghurt, chilled

Filling

1 tablespoon olive oil

2 stems spring garlic, washed and finely sliced

2 handfuls of young spinach leaves, washed and finely shredded (usually about 1 large bunch depending on where you buy it)

5 free-range egg yolks

250 g (9 oz/1 cup) sour cream

100 g (3½ oz) grated aged cheddar or parmesan

For the pastry, rub the butter into the flour and salt until it resembles breadcrumbs (or you can pulse it in a food processor). Add the yoghurt and enough ice-cold water to make a soft dough, kneading until just combined. Rest for 30 minutes, then roll out to fit a 20 cm × 6 cm (8 in × 2½ in) tin. Rest for another 30 minutes.

Preheat the oven to 180°C (350°F) and blind-bake the pastry (see Note on page 109).

To make the filling, heat the oil in a pretty big frying pan over a low heat and gently fry the garlic until it's yieldingly soft. Add the spinach and cook, stirring often, until wilted. (Popping a lid on can speed up this process.) Spread the garlic and spinach evenly over the base of the tart case. If you like, return the pan to the heat and reduce any runny cooking juices before adding to the tart.

Beat the yolks, add the sour cream and beat until just combined. Season with pepper and a little salt, remembering that the cheese is salty. Stir in three-quarters of the cheese and carefully pour this egg mixture into the tart case to fill. Top with a little more cheese.

Reheat the oven to 180°C (350°F) and bake for 12–15 minutes, or until the egg mixture has set. Serve the tart warm or at room temperature, with salad.

Pappardelle with Broad Beans and Pork Ragu

Serves 6

You could use any well-braised meat for this: lamb shoulder, osso buco, even a lightened version of Bolognese ragu, but I've used good, free-range pork in a buttery sauce for contrast with spring's gorgeous fresh broad beans.

Home-made Pasta (page 304; double the ingredients)

plain (all-purpose) flour, for dusting

200 g (7 oz) Pork Ragu (page 122), shredded

40 g (1½ oz) butter

100 g (3½ oz) double-peeled broad beans

finely grated parmesan, to serve

Roll out the pasta dough, preferably using a pasta machine, starting with two batches, to make very thin sheets. As the sheets get thinner, you will have to cut them in half, so they remain at a manageable length.

Once rolled, flour the sheets well, then cut into 20 cm (8 in) or so lengths, then fold lengthways and cut into strips about 2 cm (¾ in) wide. Gently unroll the sheets and toss very lightly in flour to avoid the pasta clumping or sticking.

Heat the ragu in a large frying pan or saucepan (big enough to toss the pasta in when cooked) with the butter. Add the broad beans, turn off the heat and leave to one side.

Cook the pasta in plenty of boiling, well-salted water until al dente. I find that with fresh egg pasta, by the time the water comes to the boil again, the pasta is cooked. Drain, but don't rinse, and leave a little water on the pasta – just a touch to help it stay moist. Add the pasta to the pork ragu and toss well to combine and evenly coat the pappardelle. Divide between six bowls, being sure that everybody gets an equal amount of sauce and broad beans. Serve with grated parmesan on the table.

Haloumi with Broad Beans, Mint and Lemon

Serves 4

Haloumi is a fabulous Cypriot-style cheese that is best served warm or it loses its magic. Fry it in a well-seasoned or non-stick pan just before serving for best results. This recipe uses boiled lemon for the dressing, but you could use preserved lemon if you have some in the fridge that needs using up.

1 whole lemon (or, if you are in a hurry, use preserved lemon and 1 tablespoon freshly squeezed lemon juice)

2 teaspoons salt

1 bay leaf

80 ml (2½ fl oz/⅓ cup) extra-virgin olive oil

1 small garlic clove, crushed

good pinch of sugar

250 g (9 oz) haloumi (drained and soaked in water if too salty)

10 g (¼ oz/½ cup) mint leaves, washed and dried, torn if big

10 g (¼ oz/½ cup) flat-leaf (Italian) parsley leaves, washed and dried

200 g (7 oz) broad beans, blanched and double peeled if necessary

Turkish-style bread, to serve

Juice the lemon and set aside 1 tablespoon juice for this dish. Keep the rest for later use. Pop the juiced halves in a small saucepan, cover with water and bring to the boil. Add the salt and bay leaf and simmer for about 1 hour, or until soft. Drain, discarding the water and bay leaf, and cut away the lemon pulp and discard. Finely dice the skin and combine with the lemon juice and 2 tablespoons of the olive oil, the garlic and sugar.

Slice the haloumi lengthways into 5 mm (¼ in) slices. Heat a seasoned or non-stick frying pan over a high heat and fry the haloumi in 1 tablespoon olive oil until browned on both sides, reducing the heat to medium if it's cooking too quickly. Drain on paper towel and keep warm.

Roughly chop the herbs. Toss the broad beans in a frying pan over a low heat with the remaining olive oil, just long enough to warm them. Lay the haloumi on a plate, toss the beans with the herbs and lemon dressing, and scatter around the haloumi. Serve immediately with lots of Turkish-style bread.

Lamb and Broad Bean Cassoulet

Serves 8

Before Columbus got confused on his voyage to India and found the Americas by mistake, France didn't have haricots or lingots, the usual cassoulet beans. Those came from the 'new world'. But in medieval times, the regions around France did have broad beans and, in some areas, they had lamb. This, then, is inspired by that time. You need to start this a day ahead to cure the lamb bellies and soften the beans, but the result is a sensational stew of a kind rarely eaten, good for early spring.

2 lamb bellies (or lamb flaps)

50 g (1¾ oz) salt, plus 1 teaspoon extra

500 g (1 lb 2 oz) dried broad beans (you can get pre-peeled dried beans from Middle Eastern supermarkets)

2 tablespoons olive oil

2 tablespoons butter (approximately)

1 kg (2 lb 3 oz) diced lamb shoulder

2 onions, peeled and diced

2 carrots, peeled and diced

2 celery stalks, diced

1 bay leaf

8–10 garlic cloves, crushed

1 tablespoon oregano, fresh if possible, or use dried Greek-style oregano on the stem

crusty bread and butter, to serve

Cure the lamb bellies by sprinkling evenly with the salt and refrigerating overnight in a covered, non-reactive dish. Soak the dried broad beans in plenty of fresh water overnight, too.

The next day, preheat the oven to 150°C (300°F) and rinse the salt from the lamb. Place in an ovenproof dish, cover with foil and bake for 2 hours, or until very tender. When cool enough to handle, pull the meat from the bones and discard the fat and any sinew or bone, but reserve the cooking juices.

In a large saucepan, warm half the oil and butter over a medium heat and fry the lamb shoulder until it's browned all over. (I do this in at least two batches.) Remove with a slotted spoon.

To the same pan, add the remaining butter and fry the onion, carrot, celery and bay leaf well until starting to colour. This may be a bit tricky depending on how much meat goop is stuck to the pan. Add the garlic and fry for another 2 minutes. Pop the lamb shoulder back into the pan and pour in enough water to just cover the meat. Use a wooden spoon to scrape any bits off the bottom of the pan, then bring to the boil. Reduce the heat to very low, add the oregano and remaining salt, and simmer, covered, for 1 hour. You can also transfer it to a 150°C (300°F) oven at this point and cook gently for 1–2 hours.

While it cooks, drain and peel the broad beans (if the skins are still a bit stuck, blanch in boiling water for a few minutes first). After an hour's cooking, stir the broad beans and roughly torn lamb belly (and its juices) into the lamb shoulder mix, and cook another hour or so until the beans are cooked, the shoulder is tender, and the liquid is low but has not reduced so much that the cassoulet is dry. Leave to sit for 10 minutes, then serve with crusty bread and butter.

Quadretti e Piselli (Peas and Fresh Pasta)

Serves 4

Square pasta (*quadretti*, sometimes called *quadrucci*) and peas (*piselli*) is typical of Italian fare, and always sounds better in Italian than English. It's deceivingly delicious for what is in it, and it celebrates what's good in the garden. Making the pasta does take a little effort, but it's worth it for a dish that simply sings spring. You can use pancetta and passata in this dish, or simplify it by removing either or even both as shown, and using just onion and peas to highlight the flavour of the fresh vegetables.

30–40 g (1–1½ oz) butter

1 small strip pancetta, cut into strips

2–3 spring onions (scallions), cleaned and sliced

80 g (2¾ oz/⅓ cup) tomato passata (puréed tomatoes)

200 g (7 oz) fresh podded peas (frozen are good out of season), or other greens such as very young, whole broad beans, sliced, or sugar-snap peas, sliced

1 quantity Home-made Pasta (page 304), rolled and cut into 1 cm (½ in) squares

80 g (2¾ oz) grated parmesan, or similar cheese

Melt the butter in a small saucepan over a low heat and fry the pancetta gently until it renders most of its fat. Add the spring onions and continue frying on a low heat for about 3 minutes until the onion is soft, but not brown. Add the passata and a couple of tablespoons of water, then the peas.

In another saucepan, bring 2 litres (68 fl oz/8 cups) well-salted water to the boil. Cook the pasta in the water until it is just cooked, stirring with a chopstick or long-handled tongs the whole time (but be careful not to shred it if you use tongs). Fresh pasta is ready pretty much as soon as the water comes back to the boil.

Scoop the pasta out (or strain through a colander, reserving a good 250 ml/8½ fl oz/1 cup of the cooking water). Add to the pea mixture, along with a little of the cooking water, and stir well to mix. You want to have a little broth in the bottom of the saucepan, so add more pasta water if it needs it. Stir through a little of the parmesan, place in serving bowls, and top with the remaining cheese to serve.

Peas, Potatoes and Bacon

Serves 6

This dish is as simple as it sounds. Its simplicity relies on the quality of the ingredients. While having good ingredients always matters, here it's paramount, because there's just no place to hide if the bacon isn't up to scratch or the peas are starchy.

150 g (5½ oz) chunk fatty bacon, cut into batons

1 kg (2 lb 3 oz) potatoes (try dutch cream), scrubbed or peeled

200 g (7 oz) fresh podded peas

Preheat the oven to 200°C (400°F).

Place the bacon on a large baking tray and roast for 10 minutes, or until well rendered, then set aside.

In the meantime, dice the potatoes into 3 cm (1¼ in) chunks. Place in a large saucepan and cover with water. Pop this over a raging flame and bring to the boil, then drain immediately. Add the spuds to the bacon tray and return the tray to the oven. Roast, stirring regularly, for about 20 minutes, or until the potatoes are cooked through and starting to colour.

To finish the dish, season with salt and pepper to taste, then stir through the peas and continue cooking for a maximum of 5 minutes, just until the peas have softened. Sometimes the heat of the spuds is enough to cook the tender spring peas without even needing to put the tray back in the oven. Stir well and serve.

Pork Ragu

Makes 700 g (1 lb 9 oz)

This makes more than you need for the pasta (page 115), but chunks can be served with baked spuds, over polenta, or shredded and frozen for future pappardelle dinners.

2–3 rosemary sprigs, roughly chopped

handful of fresh fennel tops, chopped

3 bay leaves

4 garlic cloves, peeled and chopped

500 g (1 lb 2 oz) pork shoulder meat, ideally with the skin on

olive oil, for rubbing

1 teaspoon salt

500 g (1 lb 2 oz/2 cups) tomato passata (puréed tomatoes)

Preheat the oven to 160°C (320°F).

Scatter the herbs and garlic in a roasting dish. Lay the pork on top, skin side up, rub all over with a little olive oil and season with the salt and some freshly ground black pepper. Pour the passata around the pork. Cover the dish first with baking paper, then with aluminium foil and place in the oven. Cook for at least 4 hours, or until very tender. The meat should simply fall apart.

If using for the pasta (see page 115), shred the meat with your fingers or two forks, discarding the skin, then stir through the juices from the roasting dish.

The Udder Joy of Milking

I'm often asked what is the single best thing about living and working on a farm. Eating really well is probably it. But in terms of farm work, the thing that rings my dinner bell is milking. There's a nobility in the end product, milk, which the cows produce from grass. I find this transformation utterly remarkable; Myrtle, Elsie and Florence's ability to take something we can't digest and turn it into something most of us can digest, in a matter of hours, blows my mind. Even more so, I like the way milk can be transformed in the kitchen, into cheese, butter, mascarpone, paneer and more.

So I love milk, and out on the farm, it's the cows and milking that are my labour of love. I spend about 20 hours a week, most weeks, moving cows, milking cows, cleaning the dairy. There's a deep sense of satisfaction, overlaid with greed, every morning as I ladle off the thick, rich cream from the milk. Tending cows and milking is my routine, one that I follow just about every single day. It has boundless joy, and can be both rewarding and sometimes grim.

A lactating cow is a nursing mother. At least she is on our farm, where the calves are left on for most of the lactation. From the time of conception, through her dry patch, each cow is watched and groomed. We alter her diet as she dries off, and note her every twitch when it comes close to the due date. Like any mammal, birth isn't without complication. But most of the time, nature takes its course.

But then, post birth, and in the hours afterwards, we are very much involved in the cow's life.

What is asked of a nursing mother, any nursing mother, is a lot. There's the emotional as well as physical side. There are hormonal changes, and extra risks of infection. Her nutrient needs are higher. Her mothering instinct needs to be expressed, but also managed. I do all this without the benefit of language. I don't speak the tongue of cows.

A good mother is very protective of the calf, but we also need to check the baby, and take all the surplus milk. A dairy cow, even a low-yield house cow, can easily produce four times the milk a calf will need. If you don't take that milk, the cow is prone to mastitis. And mastitis isn't just discomforting for the cow. It can kill, as we have found out all too well.

For milking, the dairy building itself is very important. We built ours with a sloping concrete floor, so it drains away when washed. The bales (the structure that locks the cow's head in place so she can't suddenly move backwards and drag off the milking machine – or drag the milking man with her) are set in one corner. She gets a feed of things she wants, and things she needs, as she's being milked. She's brushed, mollycoddled, spoilt.

And she needs to be. To get the cow to let down her milk, she needs to be relaxed, to feel comfortable. Humans are still, in some recesses of the cow's brain, a predator or a threat. We evoke a small fear in them when we move behind their shoulder, causing them to step forward. In fact, cows dominate each other in the paddock by some pretty aggressive moves, and it helps if the cows think you're the dominant one, or they'll try those aggressive moves on you. When your back is turned. It's the opposite when milking, we're trying to be their friend. More than that, we're trying to be their calf.

I wash the teats and hand milk the first little bit of milk. These tiny first few squirts are discarded, because the end of the teat is exposed to the outside world. Usually, I machine milk until the cow's empty. Occasionally I hand milk. Hand milking is quieter, more tactile, makes you more in tune with the cow's health, her mood. The machine is easier, quicker (though it takes ages to clean it afterwards), and horribly noisy. If you ever get to milk, hand milking is the romantic version to pursue. Machine milking is the practical reality that many of us come to. Begrudgingly.

I often look at the cows in my care and wish I understood them better. Their faces, to a human, are inscrutable. I watch their ears, their stance, listen to their breathing. I bond with the cows more than any other animal on the farm. I have this tactile relationship that is rare with any other animal besides a pet. I'm always hoping desperately to understand them better, and only ever really understand their otherness to me. I enjoy their company, their smell, their presence. I enjoy what they gift us, in the way of dairy, for the table. And I am always surprised and delighted when they offer it so readily most mornings of the year.

MYRTLE

Fried Flatbread with Beetroot Tops, Feta and Pine Nuts

Serves 2

The 'hungry patch' means we try to waste absolutely nothing. In some places, beetroot tops are thrown away and wasted (we sometimes feed them to the pigs) but, as a relative of silverbeet, they're perfectly edible and, in fact, quite delicious. The obvious substitute is silverbeet, or spinach if you have it.

8 beetroot (beet) tops, or use silverbeet (Swiss chard) instead

2 tablespoons butter or olive oil

1 red onion, peeled and finely sliced

2 garlic cloves, crushed

1 teaspoon whole fennel seeds (use cumin if you don't like fennel), optional

80 ml (2½ fl oz/⅓ cup) extra-virgin olive oil

4 Flatbreads (page 306)

120 g (4½ oz) goat's cheese feta

50 g (1¾ oz) toasted pine nuts

Wash the beetroot tops well, pat dry with paper towel and shred coarsely. Heat the butter in a large frying pan over a medium flame and cook the onion until browning well, about 5 minutes, stirring often. Add the garlic and cook for another minute, then add the fennel seeds and cook for a minute more. Put the leaves in (including the stems), pop a lid on and cook them right down until they're very soft. Add a little water if the pan dries before the stems have softened. Add a little pepper (the feta will probably add enough salt) and take the lid off to allow the mix to dry out a bit.

To finish the flatbread, heat some of the oil in a heavy-based frying pan with a 22 cm (8¾ in) base until warm over a medium–low heat. Add one flatbread, spread the top with half the beet-leaf mixture, dot with half the feta and sprinkle with half the pine nuts. Pop another flatbread on top and press down so that it starts to stick to the cheese as it melts. I tend to put a lid on the pan to help the mixture heat through before the bottom burns. When the bread has warmed through, remove the flatbread, add another bit of olive oil and cook the flatbread sandwich the other way up for a couple of minutes.

Remove to a plate or chopping board and leave to cool while you repeat the process with the remaining flatbread and beetroot mixture. Serve warm or at room temperature, preferably the same day.

Turnip Pasties

Serves 6

Loosely based on the Cornish pasty, this is a great way to use up turnips. We use our Hot Water Pastry (page 302) – Lard Yoghurt Pastry (page 301) is also excellent for this – and, like the traditional version, the crimped edge can be too thick to eat. In the old days, Cornish miners would use the edge to hold the pasty with their dirty hands and discard it at the end. (They also used to have a sweet filling at one end – as a bit of pudding – and a savoury filling at the other, but we don't do that.)

2 tablespoons lard, oil or butter

2 onions, peeled and cut into 5 mm (¼ in) dice

300 g (10½ oz) shin beef, diced pretty small

plain (all-purpose) flour, for dusting

1 bay leaf

1½ teaspoons salt

200 g (7 oz) starchy potato, cut into 5 mm (¼ in) dice

400 g (14 oz) European-style turnip, cut into 5 mm (¼ in) dice

1 quantity Hot Water Pastry (page 302)

1 free-range egg, lightly beaten

tomato sauce (ketchup), to serve

Warm the lard in a saucepan over a medium heat and fry the onion for about 10 minutes, or until well softened. Toss the beef in 2–3 tablespoons flour, shake off any excess, then add to the onion and cook for about 5 minutes, stirring regularly. Add 250 ml (8½ fl oz/1 cup) water, or just enough to cover the meat. Throw in the bay leaf and 1 teaspoon salt, and bring to the boil, stirring pretty much constantly to get rid of any lumps and stop it sticking. Reduce the heat to low, cover with a lid, and simmer for about 1½ hours, or until the meat is just about tender, checking that the liquid level doesn't drop too much. We actually do this long, slow cooking in a 150°C (300°F) oven on occasion.

While the meat is cooking, pop the spuds and turnips into a saucepan, cover with water, add the remaining salt and bring to the boil. Simmer for 5 minutes, then drain well. When the meat is tender, add this to the meat mixture and taste for salt and pepper. A pasty is quite pastry heavy, so make sure the filling is well seasoned. It'll be easier to make the pasties if the filling is chilled before using.

Preheat the oven to 200°C (400°F).

To make the pasties, divide the pastry into six pieces. Roll out each bit into a 20 cm (8 in) round, spoon the filling (discarding the bay leaf) onto one half, leaving room at the edge for the pastry to be sealed. Fold the pastry over, pressing it at the edges to form a half-moon shape. You can do fancy crimping on the edges, if you like.

Place the pasties on a baking tray, brush with the egg, and cook for about 30–40 minutes until the pastry is golden. Turn the oven down if they're not cooking evenly.

Serve warm with tomato sauce.

Lemon and Chilli-cured Hakurei (Japanese Turnips)

Serves 6 as a snack with drinks

We adore the crisp, sweet Japanese turnips that grow really well on the farm. They are so lovely straight from the soil, but sometimes we like to do a quick pickle, too.

250 g (9 oz) hakurei turnips

1 teaspoon salt

¼ teaspoon dried chilli flakes (optional)

finely grated zest and juice of 1 lemon

2 tablespoons fennel fronds, ideally dried and crushed, but fresh and chopped will work

Wash the turnips well, trim off the leaves (which are great in Saag Paneer, page 131), and cut into quarters.

Cure the turnips by tossing them with the salt and chilli in a bowl, then leave for 1 hour. Drain the liquid off, mix in the lemon zest, 1 teaspoon of the juice (reserve the rest for later use) and the fennel fronds. Stir to combine evenly, then allow to sit for 5 minutes before serving.

Lamb Fillets with Coriander, Mint and Lemon Marinade

Serves 3–4

This marinade is good for lamb (or hogget) chops and loin, but try splashing out on fillets to cook on the barbie for something different. We would even use diced legs or shoulder from a young animal, which have more flavour than fillets but can be more 'on the tooth'.

7 g (¼ oz/¼ cup) coriander (cilantro) leaves

5 g (¼ oz/¼ cup) mint leaves

finely grated zest and juice of ½ lemon (or use 1 teaspoon diced preserved lemon rind)

½ teaspoon ground cumin

extra-virgin olive oil

500 g (1 lb 2 oz) lamb fillets

hummus, tomato and sumac salad, and chargrilled Naan (page 307), to serve

Finely chop the herbs and mix with the lemon zest and juice, cumin, some salt and pepper and enough olive oil to make a rough paste. Rub this mixture all over the lamb and leave to marinate overnight if possible.

Heat a barbecue chargrill plate or chargrill pan over a high heat and grill the lamb for about 2–3 minutes on each side (some fillets may have three grillable sides), or until cooked how you like them. Serve with hummus, a tomato and sumac salad and chargrilled naan.

Saag Paneer

Serves 4

This is my version of the Indian classic with saag, meaning greens (and we usually have a variety), and paneer, being the fresh 'cheese' that we make in-house. We tone it down a bit in the spice department at Fat Pig because that way it marries well with our other dishes. You can spike it up more with extra chilli and garam masala if you like, especially if making a full Indian meal.

500 g (1 lb 2 oz) fresh spinach, kale, beetroot (beet) tops or, even better, a mixture, well washed and tough stalks removed

5–6 tablespoons ghee or butter

2 large onions, very thinly sliced

4 large garlic cloves, grated or crushed

4 cm (1½ in) piece of ginger, grated

1 teaspoon ground turmeric

1 large tomato, chopped, or 2–3 tablespoons tomato passata (puréed tomatoes)

1 fresh green chilli, deseeded and thinly sliced

½ teaspoon salt

2 teaspoons garam masala

2–3 tablespoons pouring (single/light) cream, yoghurt, or a little extra ghee

150 g (5½ oz) paneer, cubed (page 311)

Blanch the greens in a saucepan of boiling water for a few minutes and squeeze out any excess moisture. Chop any stalks very finely and all the leaves very roughly; you want a bit of texture to go with the smoother texture of the cheese (if using baby spinach, don't chop the leaves at all as they will break down beautifully on their own).

Heat 3–4 tablespoons of the ghee in a frying pan and fry the onion slowly over a lowish heat until starting to catch and brown – the longer you do this, the better. Add the garlic and ginger and brown a little more, for about 5 minutes. Stir in the turmeric. Continue frying, stirring constantly, to cook the turmeric without it scorching – we're talking about 30 seconds to a minute, usually. Then, add the tomato, followed by the chilli and salt. Cook for a couple of minutes, then add the greens with 2–3 tablespoons water and cook until softened.

Add the garam masala and cook gently for another 5 minutes. Taste for salt, pepper and spice. Finish with a little cream to enrich it slightly.

Heat the remaining ghee in another frying pan and fry the paneer cubes until golden. Stir the paneer into the greens and serve immediately.

Lamb Braised with Saffron in the Sardinian Style

Serves 6

I don't know where I first heard of this dish, but I was in a Sardinian frame of mind and I had lamb, I had saffron, and I had potatoes. It tastes kind of like a goulash of the Mediterranean.

2–3 tablespoons olive oil

1 kg (2 lb 3 oz) diced lamb shoulder

2 large onions, peeled and cut into rough 3 cm (1¼ in) cubes

5 garlic cloves, crushed

good handful of flat-leaf (Italian) parsley, chopped

200 ml (7 fl oz) passata (puréed tomatoes), or use tinned tomatoes and purée

generous pinch of saffron threads, ideally soaked overnight in 1 tablespoon water

2 teaspoons dried Greek oregano, or 1 tablespoon fresh oregano, chopped if leaves are big

500 g (1 lb 2 oz) waxy potatoes, peeled and cut into chunks

steamed greens, to serve

Heat 2 tablespoons of the oil in a large, heavy-based saucepan over a cracking heat, add about half the meat and brown it well. Remove with a slotted spoon and repeat with the remaining meat. Remove that too, reduce the heat to about medium and fry the onion well until just starting to brown, drizzling in more oil if needed and stirring regularly as it cooks.

Add the garlic and parsley and fry for 2 more minutes. Add the meat back to the pan with the passata, saffron, 500 ml (17 fl oz/2 cups) water and the oregano. Bring back to a simmer, scraping off any yummy brown bits from the bottom of the pan with a wooden spoon. Add salt and pepper to taste. Put a lid on and leave to simmer for about 1 hour on a very low heat. (You could do this bit in a 150°C/300°F oven, if you like.)

After an hour, add the potatoes, pushing them down into the sauce, and cook, covered, until both the potato and lamb are tender. The lamb will probably need another 30 minutes or so at least, but it does depend a lot on the age and breed of the lamb. Taste for salt and pepper and serve with steamed greens.

Smoked Paprika Gougères (Cheese Puffs)

Makes about 60 little puffs

Gougères is a posh word for cheese puffs, something light and inconsequential to eat while you have a drink. Here, we've added a little more complexity with smoked paprika. Whenever we make these, they vanish in an instant. So perhaps a double batch would be in order at the restaurant. For home use, this is a double batch.

125 g (4½ oz/½ cup) butter

1–2 teaspoons salt

¼ teaspoon smoked paprika, plus extra to serve

½ teaspoon sweet paprika

200 g (7 oz/1⅓ cups) plain (all-purpose) flour

5 free-range eggs

150 g (5½ oz) gruyère (100 g/3½ oz cut into small dice or grated, 50 g/1¾ oz finely grated)

Preheat the oven to 180°C (350°F).

Combine the butter, salt and both paprikas in a saucepan with 250 ml (8½ fl oz/1 cup) water and heat until it just comes to a simmer. Cook like a choux paste: add the flour all in one go and, straight away, stir the mixture with a wooden spoon, then vigorously stir, almost beating, over a medium heat until it's glossy and comes away from the side of the pan. Remove from the heat and beat in the eggs, one at a time, then the diced cheese and some freshly ground black pepper. The beating is really important to beat air into the puffs. You can do this bit in a freestanding electric mixer, if that's easier, using the paddle attachment.

Use two spoons to put teaspoon-sized blobs of the mixture in rows onto lined baking trays (or, alternately, pipe little balls onto baking trays), allowing room for them to double in size in the oven. Top with the remaining grated cheese, sprinkle on a touch of extra smoked paprika and bake for about 25 minutes, or until puffed and cooked through.

Serve just as they are, cool enough to handle, or even at room temperature. They store well out of the fridge in an airtight container for a day or so, but can soften a bit.

Chorizo and White Bean Soup

Serves 6–8

Good-quality chorizo has a delectable paprika hit. If yours is a bit lacking, add a touch of sweet paprika at the end of frying, too.

- 2 tablespoons olive oil or pork fat
- 100 g (3½ oz) dried chorizo, cut into 5 mm (¼ in) slices
- 2 onions, peeled and diced
- 2 carrots, washed and diced
- 3 celery stalks, diced
- 2 bay leaves
- 2 garlic cloves, crushed (optional)
- 300 g (10½ oz) dried white beans (like northern beans or haricots), soaked overnight and drained
- crusty bread, to serve
- extra-virgin olive oil, for drizzling

Warm the oil in a very large saucepan over a high heat and cook the chorizo until it starts to surrender its fat and brown a little. Remove with a slotted spoon, eat a piece or two, then save the rest for later.

Reduce the heat to fairly low, then fry the onion in the same pan, in the rendered fat until soft. Add the carrot, celery and bay leaves and fry well without colouring much. If the chorizo isn't very garlicky, add the garlic at the end of the frying time, too.

Add the rinsed white beans, all the remaining chorizo that you haven't eaten and 2 litres (68 fl oz/8 cups) water and simmer for 1½ hours, or until the beans are as tender as a broken heart. Taste for salt and pepper and serve with crusty bread and a drizzle of extra-virgin olive oil.

Cotechino with Lentils

Serves at least 4

The small, bluey-green kind of lentil makes the perfect accompaniment for sausages. Other lentils just don't work as well. Make a bigger batch and freeze leftovers for midweek meals. Cotechino is a big sausage made using pork skin in part, so it's usually boiled before being sliced and fried. Seek it out in good butchers, or use a pure pork sausage in this recipe instead.

1–2 tablespoons olive oil, plus extra for frying

50 g (1¾ oz) speck, bacon or pancetta, cut into bite-sized batons

1 onion, peeled and finely diced

1 garlic clove, crushed

2–3 tablespoons white wine

200 g (7 oz) small, French-style green lentils

2 thyme sprigs

1 bay leaf

4 big or 8 smaller slices cotechino, boiled and skinned

Warm the oil in a saucepan over a modest heat. Fry the speck for a couple of minutes until the fat starts to melt out. Add the onion and fry until soft, and perhaps starting to colour slightly. Toss in the garlic and cook for another minute. Turn up the heat, slosh in the white wine and boil for 1 minute. Add the lentils, 1 litre (34 fl oz/4 cups) water, the thyme and bay leaf and simmer gently for about 30 minutes, checking that the lentils remain just below the level of the liquid so they cook evenly. Put a lid on if you want. The lentils should be soft rather than crunchy, but not falling apart either. Turn up the heat when they're just about done and boil rapidly to reduce the liquid until it's just a dribble to moisten the lentils. Add some salt and pepper to taste.

Pan-sear the cotechino in a minimum of oil until well browned on either side. It tends to spit like an angry sow when it's being cooked because of the skin content of the sausage, so a lid is helpful to avoid oil splashes and burns. Serve the lentils hot with cotechino, or perhaps with slow-roasted duck. Leftover lentils make a cracker of a lunch with a poached egg, too.

Panada (Sardinian-style Lamb, Potato and Saffron Pie)

Serves 8

This pie, which uses the same fabulous pastry I like to use for pork pies, owes its heritage to the island of Sardinia, off the Italian west coast. Historically isolated and intrinsically rural, Sardinians often cook very simple, homely dishes based on lamb and spuds. You can cut the top off this pie and save all the cooking juices, or cut it on a plate to do the same. You could allow it to cool fully before slicing, or make smaller, individual pies and bake them for about 50 minutes instead.

750 g (1 lb 11 oz) lamb shoulder, cut into 1 cm (½ in) dice

12 sundried tomatoes, thinly sliced

2 tablespoons extra-virgin olive oil

1 small bunch flat-leaf (Italian) parsley, leaves only, chopped

4–5 garlic cloves, crushed

pinch of saffron threads

1 tablespoon salt

750 g (1 lb 11 oz) potatoes, sliced about 5 mm (¼ in) thick

1 quantity Hot Water Pastry (page 302)

1 free-range egg, whisked with a pinch of salt and 1 teaspoon water

Daikon, Fennel and Kohlrabi Slaw (page 56), to serve (optional)

Mix the lamb, sundried tomatoes, oil, parsley, garlic and saffron in a bowl and leave to infuse in the fridge (ideally overnight but a few hours is usually sufficient).

When ready to cook, preheat the oven to 180°C (350°F). Toss the lamb mix with the salt and potatoes (I like to add some black pepper at this stage, too). Roll out three-quarters of the pastry to fit a 23 cm (9 in) wide, 6 cm (2½ in) deep pie dish or cake tin, making sure it overhangs by about 2 cm (¾ in). Fill with the lamb and spud mixture, pressing well into the edge and base of the tin. You really want a compact filling. Roll out the remaining pastry to make a lid and squeeze the edges together tightly to seal. Roll this squeezed pastry over so that it curls on the inside of the tin, working in circular motion to form a good solid rim of pastry. Cut a small slit in the top, then brush all over the top with the egg wash.

Bake in the centre of the oven for 30 minutes, then reduce the heat to 160°C (320°F) and bake for a further 1 hour. Keep an eye on it so that it doesn't brown too much, turning down the heat to 150°C (300°F) if necessary. The pastry should be golden and the filling bubbling a bit. Remove from the oven and leave to sit for a good hour before serving, remembering that the cooking juices will spill out everywhere even then. Or take it on a picnic and serve it after it cools to room temperature. Daikon, Fennel and Kohlrabi Slaw (page 56) makes a nice accompaniment.

Ciccioli and Rosemary Pizza

Makes 4 pizzas

Ciccioli are the crunchy bits you get when you render pork fat. The best stuff comes from the fat around the kidneys, which forms this lacy mass when you cook it down and pour off the molten lard. The golden-brown crunchy bits are incredibly flavoursome, and here they lift a pizza dough out of the ordinary.

100 g (3½ oz) pork renderings, blitzed crackling, or similar

1 quantity Pizza Dough (page 303), made but not rolled a second time

plain (all-purpose) flour, for dusting

1 tablespoon pork fat, melted

1 rosemary sprig

salt flakes, for sprinkling

Divide the renderings and the pizza dough into four and knead the renderings into the pieces of dough. Cover them and leave to rise, at room temperature or a bit warmer, for an hour or so, until doubled in size.

Preheat the oven to maximum heat. If you have a big pizza tile or stone, place it in the oven for 30 minutes.

On well-floured pizza trays, push the dough out to make rounds using your floured fingertips and spinning the trays to press the dough into even circle shapes. You can roll the dough instead, but that will just push out all the air, so it's best to shape it with your fingers. Once your pizza bases are the right size and shape – about 25 cm (10 in) diameter is good – brush with pork fat, add a few leaves rosemary, and sprinkle with salt.

Bake in the centre of the hot oven for 3–5 minutes, depending on how hot it is, or even longer, until starting to brown. If you're using the hot tile, slide the pizza off the tray onto the tile to cook without removing the tile from the oven. Serve the pizza when cool enough to handle.

Anchovy Sable

Makes approx. 35

These savoury shortbreads are quite moreish, so you'll never be able to stop at just one. Add more anchovy if you want them to have a saltier zing.

150 g (5½ oz/1 cup) plain (all-purpose) flour

140 g (5 oz) unsalted butter, chilled and cubed

40 g (1½ oz) parmesan, finely grated

30 g (1 oz) anchovies, very finely chopped

1 tablespoon poppy seeds

olives, to serve (optional)

Tip the flour into a large bowl and rub in the butter until it resembles fine breadcrumbs. Stir in the cheese, then add the anchovies and gently mix together to make a firm dough.

Alternatively, you could do this in a food processor by adding the flour, butter and cheese, then pulsing until fine before adding the anchovies and pulsing again until the mixture just comes together.

Either way, once it's done and you have a manageable dough, roll it into a log about 4 cm (1½ in) wide. You can cut this log in half to make it easier to manage if you need to. Roll the log in the poppy seeds. Wrap in plastic wrap and pop in the fridge to chill for 30 minutes.

Preheat the oven to 200°C (400°F).

Using a sharp knife, cut the unwrapped, chilled log into slices about ½ cm (¼ in) thick, to make around 35 biscuits in total. Place the biscuits on a lined baking tray, leaving a little room between each to allow for spreading when baking. Bake for 10 minutes, or until just starting to turn golden. Transfer to a wire rack to cool.

Store in an airtight container for 2–3 days or simply just eat them all in one great big sitting. Then think about eating a carrot for your health.

The Harvest & The Surfeit

There's something primal about touching the earth. So many people get so much joy from the simple act of growing their own food when they obviously don't have to work the land in order to feed themselves. Others grow things for the beauty they create, not the dinners they make, and tend ornamental gardens. For many, communing with nature can be as simple as sticking a trowel in the ground and loosening a few radishes to have before dinner. For us, this connection to soil is on a bigger scale, but no different at its heart.

If you grow food, harvesting is a joy and a responsibility. While growing food is one thing, it's another to ensure it is picked at ultimate ripeness, at the right time, not only of the year or the month, but the right time of the day in some cases. The art of harvest is to capture the food at its ultimate. There's little point in creating a Garden of Eden if you're not there to catch the apple as it drops.

I'm not very good at the harvest. Mornings and afternoons spent with cows and pigs, days spent in the kitchen – these mean that the food I harvest often goes straight into my mouth. I gobble more raspberries than I put in the bucket. I'm entranced by the scent that rises as I pull a carrot from the ground. And then I eat it. I love the fragrance in the hot house all year, but particularly in tomato season. This, plus the manual labour, makes me hungry. I'm not a reliable person on the harvest.

A bountiful garden is a boon to the kitchen. Until it overwhelms. Knowing the effort that goes into growing things makes us very conscious of waste. Sure, the garden waste can generally be fed to pigs, or chooks, or even used to feed worms, but food that's good enough for humans we try our best to use. Very little is wasted. Some is pickled. Some fermented. Some is frozen, or dehydrated, or bottled. And a tiny bit might get sold off site.

The surfeit is both a blessing and a curse. To ensure we have enough food for every week, we have to produce more than enough. More than enough for our family and our guests. The garden is always planning for a glitch in nature; perhaps frost, or hail, or pests or storms, which may damage our harvest. So, in the absence of that glitch, we have more food than we can use on any particular week. The trick is to use that for festivals. For extra events, to feed the staff, our neighbours, or our community.

There's joy in the stripping and hanging of the garlic crop; hundreds of the bulbs drying in the hay shed for other times. We are overwhelmed at times, and find new ways with old ingredients. Fresh zucchini flowers come on so thick and fast that we're always playing with ways to use them. This year Rob, our cook, decided to stuff them with homemade ricotta, scented with crumbled pork crackle, and serve them antipasto style.

Tomatoes become passata, sauce, chutney and relish. Cucumbers become gherkins or bread and butter pickles. Apples turn into syrup, cider, pie, tarte tatin, pudding and cake.

The glut is the great joy, and the great weight of responsibility of the kitchen. Capturing the flavour of each season, and preserving it for other times, is one of the many true pleasures of living on the land.

Lemon Posset

Serves 6

A posset is a curdled or set cream (hence the term's use with babies and what they leave behind on your shoulder when you burp them). It is so easy to make, and yet so delicious to eat – like a British version of panna cotta. The heating of the cream along with the acid in the lemon juice help to set it into a lovely pudding. It keeps rather well in the fridge when covered, so can be stored for 3–4 days before serving, but a day after making it's at its best.

600 ml (20½ fl oz) pouring (single/light) cream

150 g (5½ oz) sugar

zest and strained juice of 2 lemons

fresh fruit or brandied kumquats, to serve (optional)

In a saucepan, combine the cream and sugar and boil for 3 minutes.

Cool, then whisk through the zest and juice. Pour into six serving dishes. Cover the possets and pop into the fridge for a few hours, ideally overnight, before serving.

When ready to serve, you leave it as is, or serve with a little fresh fruit, or some brandied kumquats, or similar.

Sour Milk and Raspberry Cake

Serves 12

Soured milk makes this cake so much better than normal milk. If you don't have some that's just turned, use a bit of buttermilk, yoghurt, some kefir, or a good tablespoon of lemon juice to help sour the mix. We use the last of the frozen raspberries, but you can substitute chunks of baked quince or poached pear for the raspberries if you like.

250 g (9 oz/1 cup) butter, softened, plus extra for greasing

345 g (12 oz/1½ cups) caster (superfine) sugar

3 free-range eggs

1 teaspoon vanilla extract

250 ml (8½ fl oz/1 cup) sour milk

400 g (14 oz/2⅔ cups) self-raising flour

100 g (3½ oz) frozen raspberries, plus extra to serve

clotted or whipped cream, to serve

Preheat the oven to 180°C (350°F). Grease and line a 26 cm (10¼ in) round springform cake tin.

Beat the butter and sugar until light and pale. (When it's cold weather, I sometimes soften the butter in the oven very carefully first, as it makes it easier to beat.) Beat in the eggs, one at a time, then add the vanilla, then the milk and flour in two alternating batches, stirring just until the batter's combined. (I like to add a touch more than the cup of milk.) Stir in the still-frozen raspberries and pour the batter into the prepared tin.

Bake for about 35–45 minutes, or until a skewer inserted in the middle of the cake comes out clean. Cool on a rack for 10 minutes, then remove from the tin and finish cooling on the rack before serving or storing in an airtight container. The cake is nice with a few extra berries, softened on the stove then poured over, and perhaps clotted or just simple whipped cream for serving.

Mushroom and Lentil Non-Shepherd's Pie

Serves 8

I know, it's not a shepherd's pie without lamb, but I wanted a meat substitute and love the potato topping. Maybe it's a 'pulse grower's' pie, but that name really lacks a certain romance.

150 g (5½ oz) butter

2 tablespoons olive oil

2 onions, peeled and finely chopped

2 carrots, peeled and finely chopped

2 thyme sprigs

2 bay leaves

500 g (1 lb 2 oz) button mushrooms, chopped

3–4 dried mushrooms, soaked and chopped

1 teaspoon salt

80 g (2¾ oz/⅓ cup) tomato passata (puréed tomatoes), or similar

2–3 tablespoons Worcestershire sauce, or more to taste

200 g (7 oz) cooked green lentils (about 100 g/3½ oz before cooking)

750 g (1 lb 11 oz) cooked potato (I like dutch cream), mashed or put through a ricer

100 g (3½ oz) grated cheddar, or similar cheese

2–3 tablespoons grated horseradish

steamed green veg, to serve (optional)

Heat 50 g (1¾ oz) of the butter and the olive oil in a large, heavy-based saucepan over a medium heat and fry the onion and carrot well with the thyme and bay leaves. Cook until the onion starts to brown, then add the mushrooms and reserve the soaking water. Continue frying until the onions start to break down, adding the salt to help them soften. And some pepper, which I think is good at this stage. When the onions and mushrooms are soft, pour in the mushroom soaking water, the passata, Worcestershire and lentils. Cook well for about 10 minutes to create a thick, flavoursome stew, then pour into an ovenproof casserole dish.

Preheat the oven to 180°C (350°F).

Mix hot, just-mashed spuds with the remaining butter, cheese and horseradish. Smother this mixture over the pie and bake for about 40 minutes, or until golden and steaming. Serve as is, or with some steamed green veg.

Walnut Shortbread Biscuits

Makes approx. 35

These are wonderful shortbreads with the scent of walnut. Now that's what I call a biscuit. If you don't have a cutter, simply make squares.

- 125 g (4½ oz/1 cup) walnuts, freshly shelled if possible
- 180 g (6½ oz) butter, softened
- 50 g (1¾ oz) caster (superfine) sugar
- 25 g (1 oz) soft brown sugar
- 1 tablespoon good-quality honey
- 200 g (7 oz/1⅓ cups) plain (all-purpose) flour, plus extra for dusting
- 50 g (1¾ oz) cornflour (cornstarch)

Preheat the oven to 180°C (350°F).

Place the walnuts on a baking tray and toast in the oven until they start to colour ever so slightly and become fragrant. Keep an eye on them, as they burn quickly. Remove from the oven and allow to cool slightly. Place the cooled walnuts on a sheet of baking paper then fold the paper over the top and gently crush the nuts with a rolling pin. Aim for a fairly fine crush, but some larger pieces are okay.

In a large bowl or the bowl of a freestanding electric mixer, cream the butter, sugars and honey until pale. Fold in the crushed walnuts, then the flours and mix until just combined, being careful not to overmix. It's okay if it's still a bit crumbly. Turn the dough out onto a lightly floured bench and gently knead just until smooth. Don't overdo it, or the final biscuits can become a bit tough. Pat into a round disc and, if it's feeling a bit too soft and sticky, refrigerate for 20 minutes or so.

Once cool, roll out the dough onto a lightly floured surface to about 4 mm (¼ in) thick and, using a 5 cm (2 in) round cutter, cut out circles and place them on a lined baking tray, allowing a little space between each one.

Bake for about 12 minutes – you only want them slightly coloured on the edges – then remove from oven. They will feel soft but will firm up as they cool.

Store in an airtight container for up to 3 days.

Strawberries with Yoghurt Cream and Rose Geranium Butter Biscuits

Serves 6

A lovely buttery biscuit matched with the first of the strawberries that are warmed by the sun then on the stove? Sign me up now.

250 g (9 oz/1⅔ cups) strawberries, tops removed and cut in half if needed

2 tablespoons honey

200 g (7 oz) Greek yoghurt

100 g (3½ oz) thick (double/heavy) cream

1 quantity Rose Geranium Butter Biscuits (below) or Walnut Shortbread Biscuits (page 149)

Pop the strawberries into a small saucepan with 1 tablespoon honey, place over an itsy-bitsy flame and gently warm for just 1 minute. You don't want to cook the berries completely, just take the raw edge off.

In the meantime, whisk the yoghurt with the cream and remaining honey in a large bowl until combined and thick.

To serve, get six plates and dob a tiny bit of the yoghurt cream in the middle to stop the biscuits slipping. Top each with a biscuit, spread generously with the yoghurt cream and garnish with a few strawberries so they're evenly distributed across all six plates. Drizzle with any juices, and top with the remaining biscuits. Serve immediately with a sticky wine.

Rose Geranium Butter Biscuits

Makes approx. 12

Rose geranium is one of those incredible culinary herbs that just does wonders for desserts. Here, the gentle aroma is used to add sparkle to shortbread-style biscuits that can be used to sandwich just-warmed strawberries. In the place of geranium, if you haven't got yourself a plant, use a few drops of rosewater instead.

200 g (7 oz) butter, softened

120 g (4½ oz) caster (superfine) sugar

2 free-range egg yolks

1 teaspoon vanilla extract

3–4 rose geranium leaves, finely shredded

270 g (9½ oz/2 cups) plain (all-purpose) flour, plus extra for dusting

Beat the butter with the sugar until smooth, then beat in the eggs. You don't need it too light and fluffy, but well beaten nonetheless. Once the eggs are incorporated, fold in the vanilla and geranium. Next, fold in the flour until only just combined, then cover and refrigerate the mixture for 30 minutes.

Preheat the oven to 180°C (350°F).

On a floured bench, roll the dough about 5 mm (¼ in) thick, and cut into 6 cm (2½ in) or similar-sized rounds using a biscuit cutter. Lay these rounds out neatly on a baking tray lined with baking paper. You'll probably need two trays, actually.

Bake for 12–15 minutes, or until just starting to colour but not brown at all. Cool on the tray for a few minutes, then transfer to a wire rack to cool completely. The biscuits can be stored for a couple of days in an airtight container.

Lemon Lime Delicious

Serves 2–6, depending on sweet tooths

I normally make a straight lemon delicious, but this makes a lovely change. It can be sprightly with acid, so if you don't want it quite as tart, cut the limes down to just two.

50 g (1¾ oz) butter, softened, plus extra for greasing

130 g (4½ oz) caster (superfine) sugar

50 g (1¾ oz/⅓ cup) plain (all-purpose) flour, sifted

pinch of salt

grated zest and juice of 2 lemons

grated zest and juice of 3 limes

500 ml (17 fl oz/2 cups) full-cream (whole) milk

4 free-range eggs, separated

vanilla ice cream, to serve

Cream the butter and sugar in a bowl until light and fluffy, then fold in the flour and salt. Fold in the lemon and lime zest and juice, and stir in the milk (the mixture should be quite runny). Fold in the lightly beaten egg yolks.

Whip the egg whites to snow (I love that old-fashioned term – it just means soft peaks). Fold one-quarter of the egg white into the lemon mix to lighten, then fold in the remaining egg white.

Preheat the oven to 180°C (350°F).

Pour the batter into a greased 2 litre (68 fl oz/8 cup) casserole dish and place the dish in a roasting tin. Pour in enough hot water to come two-thirds of the way up the side of the dish (this is more water than most recipes call for).

Bake for 40–50 minutes, or until the top is golden. Allow to cool for 30 minutes before serving (it will sag as though it's disconsolate, but that's perfectly normal, and it's really quite a cheery dish).

Serve with loads of vanilla ice cream.

Spotted Dick

Serves 6–8

Traditionally a steamed suet pudding with raisins or currants in it, spotted dick is so called – at least in part – because of the dried fruit. My version is a simple but quite scrumptious butter version. It's quite hard to tip from the bowl to see the raisins, but it could be worth a try, if you like. Substitute muscatels for the raisins to be a little bit posh.

120 g (4½ oz) butter, softened, plus extra for greasing

150 g (5½ oz) raisins, soaked in brandy to soften for a few hours, if you like

200 g (7 oz) caster (superfine) sugar, plus extra for lining the bowl

grated zest of 1 lemon and ½ orange

1 free-range egg

200 g (7 oz/1⅓ cups) self-raising flour

125 ml (4 fl oz/½ cup) full-cream (whole) milk

good-quality cream or custard, to serve

Butter a 2 litre (68 fl oz/8 cup) pudding bowl or similar really well. Press a few of the raisins around the side to create a nice spotted effect once the pudding is unmoulded if you want to give that a crack. Sprinkle the tin with a tiny bit of caster sugar too, to help prevent sticking.

Cream the butter and sugar with both zests until pale. Beat in the egg, then fold in half the flour and half the milk until smooth, then repeat with the remaining flour and milk. Stir in the remaining raisins.

Tip the pudding batter into the pudding bowl and seal with the lid. (If you don't have a pudding bowl, use a heatproof bowl and cover the top with plastic wrap and then foil, then tie tightly around the rim to seal and make a handle from the string. This will make it easier to retrieve the pudding from the saucepan later.)

Place the pudding bowl in a large saucepan and pour in enough hot water to reach one-third of the way up the side of the bowl. Bring to a simmer, cover with a tight-fitting lid and steam for about 2 hours, checking occasionally that there's enough water in the pan.

Very gingerly remove the pudding bowl from the water, take the lid off and serve.

If you're really keen, you can try to turn it out. Run a knife around the bowl to help make sure the pudding is loosened. Tip the pud' onto a plate and serve warm with good cream or a custard.

Golden Syrup and Macadamia Tart

Serves 10–12

This tart, made from pretty much everything we don't grow for a change, is a lovely variation on one we do with honey. We make it because, well, it's so damn good, and we're not harvesting fruit in spring. That's our excuse, anyway. The nuts go almost nougat-like with the buttery syrup, and you only need a thin slice to make you feel like the world is a better place.

1 quantity Shortcrust Pastry (see below)

150 g (5½ oz) butter, plus extra for greasing

50 g (1¾ oz) sugar

100 g (3½ oz) golden syrup

80 ml (2½ fl oz/⅓ cup) pouring (single/light) cream

3 tablespoons grated orange zest

250 g (9 oz) unsalted macadamia nuts

200 g (7 oz) slivered almonds

Shortcrust pastry

200 g (7 oz/1⅓ cups) plain (all-purpose) flour, plus extra for dusting

120 g (4½ oz) butter, chilled and diced

1 tablespoon caster (superfine) sugar

1 free-range egg yolk

1 tablespoon iced water

Grease a 27 cm (10¾ in) round flan tin with a removable base.

To make the pastry, pulse the flour, butter and sugar in a food processor until just combined and the mixture resembles breadcrumbs. Pulse in the egg yolk and enough water to combine. Tip the pastry onto a clean bench and press together to make a ball. Wrap tightly in plastic wrap and refrigerate to rest for 30 minutes.

Roll out the pastry on a well-floured bench and use it to line the prepared flan tin. Prick the base with a fork, then cover and rest in the fridge for a further 30 minutes.

Preheat the oven to 180°C (350°F) and blind-bake the pastry (see Note on page 109). Leave to cool slightly, keeping the oven on.

Heat the butter, sugar, golden syrup and cream in a large saucepan and simmer for 3 minutes. Add the zest and simmer for another minute. Fold through the nuts and spread evenly over the cooked pastry case.

Bake for 25–35 minutes, or until the top is a nice caramel colour. Cool for several minutes in the tin before removing. Store in an airtight container in the fridge, but serve at room temperature.

Garibaldi Biscuits

Makes 20

My niece Stephanie dictated this family recipe to her grandma to send in an email to me, keeping the old favourites alive.

30 g (1 oz) butter

120 g (4½ oz) self-raising flour, plus extra for dusting

pinch of salt

30 g (1 oz) caster (superfine) sugar

2 tablespoons milk

90 g (3 oz) currants

Rub the butter into the flour and salt until it's fairly even, without any big lumps of butter. Stir in the sugar, then add the milk, kneading by hand to create a slightly stiff dough.

Preheat the oven to 180°C (350°F).

Turn this onto a floured board, pat lightly into a square shape and roll out very evenly to about 3–4 mm (⅛ in) thick. Cut the dough in half, sprinkle one half evenly with the currants, and cover with the other half of the dough. Roll the mixture again until 3–4 mm (⅛ in) thick, keeping it as square as possible.

Trim the edges, then cut the dough into squares or triangles and bake on a lined tray for 8–12 minutes.

Smoking Bishop

Smoking Bishop is a mulled port drink mentioned in Charles Dickens' classic book, *A Christmas Carol*, where a reformed Ebenezer Scrooge shared a glass with Bob Cratchit by the fire. Traditionally, oranges and lemons were used, but we have kumquats in the kitchen, so we used them instead. If you can't find kumquats, revert to the original and use one orange and one lemon, stud with cloves, roast whole, then slice before adding to the bishop. We were introduced to this drink by our friend and co-conspirator Michelle Crawford. Oh, and the name? Supposedly the port wine resembles a bishop's purple robes and the smoke refers to the steam rising from the smoking-hot drink in your glass. This makes quite a large quantity, but you can always pour any extra in glass bottles and store in the fridge for weeks, and gently reheat in a saucepan as required.

8 kumquats

1 tablespoon whole cloves

750 ml (25½ fl oz/3 cups) medium-bodied red wine, such as pinot noir

115 g (4 oz/½ cup) brown sugar

5 cinnamon sticks

3 star anise

8 whole allspice berries

750 ml (25½ fl oz/3 cups) port

Preheat the oven to 180°C (350°F).

Stud each kumquat with three or four cloves, then place the kumquats in an ovenproof dish and bake until just softened and a little browned, about 10 minutes.

Place half the red wine, the sugar, cinnamon sticks, any remaining cloves, star anise and allspice berries in a large saucepan over a low heat and stir until the sugar has dissolved. Let the mixture simmer on a low heat for 1 hour. If you're an organised sort of person, you could begin this recipe the day before and remove from the heat at this point to let the mixture infuse, covered, overnight at room temperature before starting on the next bit.

Add the port and the remaining red wine to the spiced hot wine mixture. Stir to combine and heat until the mixture is 'smoking' hot, being careful not to let it boil or you'll lose much of the alcohol and some of the flavour. When ready to serve, strain (if desired) the smoking bishop into a serving bowl (or just serve straight from the saucepan for a casual effect), adding the baked cumquats and any juices.

Ladle into warmed glasses or teacups and serve by the fire.

As spring races to its end, the first of the summer fruit has us going all giddy with joy.

Summer

Berries
Sun-baked stone fruit
The longest day
Brown grass
Ice cream and iced sherbet
Cutting hay
River swims
Cold drinks
Cherry pit spitting competitions
Broad-brimmed hats
A glut
Tomatoes, zucchini, eggplants, capsicums
Afternoons at the beach
Blue days
Hot
Snakes
Cold towels, big fans
Berry jam
Fire bans
Harvesting, harvesting, harvesting

•

Recipes

It tightens. The soil tightens as it dries. Our smiles tighten with the sun and the heat, despite wide-brimmed hats and slip-slop-slapping with sunscreen. The plants tighten their grip on each precious drop of rain. We hang on tight and get ready for the rollercoaster ride of the busiest of seasons.

It's not just the tourist season that makes us get our skates on. Around here, the warmer months are the bountiful months. Yes, some of the surfeit carries on until autumn, but in summer, each week a fruit tends to hit peak ripeness. Each day there's something else to cook, cure or preserve. Each warm afternoon intensifies the colour and flavour of the raspberries, strawberries and currants, their slow ripening times in our cool climate the secret to their intense flavour.

It's hard to keep the garden watered come summer. The crisping of the grass means the hay season is upon us, but in our vegie beds, the drying wind and days of ceaseless sun can roast things on the vine or in the plot. If we're not careful, the seedlings can wilt and the berries desiccate. The gardeners, too, must be wise to water, drinking steadily and resting in the hottest parts of the day under the shade of the trees.

Summer means trips to the river to swim. It means wallows for pigs. It means long, really long, days where the sun rises well before we want to rise, and the dusk usually settles well after we retire. On the longest day, in late December, you can be pulling a flathead from the river at 10 pm and not need a torch to remove the hook. Apparently. I say apparently because I am no fisherman.

Fruit is poached. Jam is set. Jars are filled with myriad styles of cucumber pickle: fermented or vinegared, a taste of summer stored for the months to come. We make berry shrub from brambles; the fruit from a tangled mix of loganberry, boysenberry and youngberry canes is turned into a cider vinegar–based cordial the colour of a vibrant red wine.

Our herb garden leaps to life after the dormancy of the cold. Lovage stands tall with its hollow stalks and aromatic serrated leaves. There's chamomile, river mint, lemon verbena, lemon balm, tarragon and chives. Nadia, our gardener, has let the parsnip go to seed. It shoots up tall on stiff russet stems. Like fennel and lovage, its flowers are huge yellow umbels, the umbrella-shaped crowns made up of multiple flowers. We do it because it attracts insects. Because we may save the seed. Because it looks damned pretty in the garden, and a cheery garden is an even happier place than a normal garden.

Our first rockmelons appear, but only the charentais are worth the wait. The others, less fragrant and less sweet, make delightful sorbet. The French-developed charentais, however, make my knees go weak. They're the kind of melon you can't put in the car when the windows are up, they're so perfumed. The kind that goes incredibly well with our prosciutto. The kind money can't buy. They make me think of how much a garden embellishes your life. The joy of the growing, the harvesting, the eating that no amount of money can imitate. Standing in the garden as the sun dips beneath the horizon, after a long day on the farm, gobbling raspberries with gay abandon, giggling like a schoolboy before moseying back to the house for the sleep of a labourer ... money can't buy gleefulness like that.

The Summer

We race to keep up at this time of year. Summer is the time of plenty. While some crops span into autumn, the peak is now for berries, beans, cucumbers, zucchini, eggplant and capsicum. We get a sprinkling of tomatoes. It's now that we must deal with stone fruit, from our farm and those around us (neighbours call with offers of plums, cherries, nectarines, boxes and boxes of them). Summer gardens are full of work, taking more water, more time to pick the crop, and they give more work to the kitchen in terms of preserving. We want nothing to go to waste, and so harvest we must.

Harvest

December.
Zucchini (courgettes), raspberries and strawberries, brambleberries: loganberries, youngberries, boysenberries. Currants. Rhubarb, gooseberries, sugar snaps, snow peas (mangetout), garlic. The first baby carrots.

January.
The first tomatoes from the greenhouse. Cucumbers, padrón peppers. Herbs: anise hyssop, varieties of oregano, marjoram, thyme and lemon thyme, basil. Green beans, zucchini, tomatillos, apricots, peaches, cherries.

February.
Capsicums (bell peppers) and chillies – Alma paprika, corno di toro, jimmy nardello. Eggplants (aubergines). The first few ears of corn, including multi-coloured flint corn. Outside tomatoes and cucumbers, runner beans. Our first ever rockmelon (cantaloupe). Nectarines. The first good apples, the Gravensteins. Plums.

A full greenhouse, bountiful with so much that relies on a hotter climate than ours.

12
DECEMBER

Weather. I'm a weather bore. Here in Tassie, so are many others. It defines much of what people do. The forecast is all about sheep graziers, the size of the swells, the strength of coastal winds for fishermen, and occasional bushwalker alerts.

Farmers, by definition, are obsessed with the weather, by what happens in the skies. Because how Mother Nature treats us determines how we manage our land, rear our crops, grow food for you to eat. Farmers – alchemists who turn sunlight, soil and air into nourishment for the rest of the world – rely on what nature throws at them.

Right now, it's throwing good things. Mild, with enough moisture in the soil for the grass, and there hasn't been a frost for months. The garden is booming. Groaning, really. Zucchini have raced to the table. The strawberries have started in earnest. And the paddocks are long and lush, the perfect way for things to be before the big dry of the next few months, when grass stagnates. There's a thick wodge of cream on the milk, thanks to a surfeit of clover. The long grass is a veritable playground for the pigs. Fruit is already fattening on the trees, small orbs drinking in the sunshine.

The rains, if this year follows the pattern, have gone for the next few months. The wettest time is winter, the driest when we need the rain the most. For the start of the dry, our dams are full, the grass long, our animals fat. We head into summer buoyed with possibility.

9 JANUARY

Hay's in. The leggy grass, if cut at just the right time, stores its goodness for leaner months. If left to stagnate, it forms seeds, then returns to the atmosphere once again. If we can graze it, trample it to the ground, or turn it into hay, we've stashed carbon away for another day.

This is the first year we've pulled in hay without the threat of a storm. Strange, but true: in this driest of seasons usually the last decent rain of the summer is on the horizon as the hay baler rounds into the paddocks. Not this year, for the first time in the seven we've lugged hay. We enlist Rob, our new cook, on his second week, and Rowan, our farmhand, to help toss bales, stack bales, move bales, at the start of a long day on the farm. Five hundred bales later, the sheds are full. Money in the bank is how a farmer sees hay, once you're over the itchy arms, the deep exhaustion from lifting bale after bale overhead and tossing them onto the ute. It's a good tiredness. A virtuous fatigue, born of simple, hard labour.

We suck down water, litres of the stuff. We scoff fruitcake, Christmas leftovers, between loads. We have long since learnt to close our mouths and eyes when we move hay bales, to protect our sight and avoid choking on the stuff. I love the sweet smell of hay. I love the neatness of paddocks when the bales lie there catching the last of the sun's rays. I love the muskiness of the hay shed. And I love the sleep that comes from an honest day's work on the farm.

22 JANUARY

The heat brings new harvests. Our eggplants are sublime. Dark, purple, stained with stripes, fat and thin varieties, some shaped like a rotund clown, some long and curved back like a gymnast. The zucchini give and give and give. We stuff their fresh flowers with house-made ricotta enriched with cream and scented with herbs. We roast tomatillos until they're dark, blacken onions and bake whole bulbs of garlic to flavour them with. Add some dried oregano and paprika and you've got a salsa.

Cucumber flowers, precious as pearls to us, make a singular visit to the table: a fleeting appearance one lunch of the year, their elegant flavour as much about captured sunshine as it is about cucumber.

In our hearts we know summer will look like this, with parched soil and dry grass. But it still surprises each year. As we tick off more and more years on the land, the seasons continue to creep up on us. In summer we can't quite believe that, come winter, the paddocks will become boggy and the driveway turn into a creek. But equally, in the emerald green of spring, summers past seem calmer, less arid, more lush in hindsight than they were at the time. That's what we love about this place. One of the many things, anyway: the endlessness of seasonal change. The astonishment and wonderment at the passing of time as the light changes and the earth moves and the plants and birds and wildlife tell us that, yes, it is summer once more and it is a time of low rain and higher temperatures. It is a time of bounty that has to be preserved for leaner months.

Peaches fall from the tree. The first apples, the early season Vista Bella and Gravenstein and Beauty of Bath are all so ripe they start to drop faster than we can pick them. These windfalls are fed to pigs, some to the cattle as a sweet treat. The peaches, well, if we get to them the same day, these are peaches as nature intended them to be. As sweet and fragrant as is possible, because that gives the seed deep within the melting flesh the best chance at germinating. And this flesh is the peach of our dreams. The sort you eat over the bathtub. The kind you giggle at while you eat. They're so good that Nadia, our gardener, rates this time of year the best of all to be making clandestine trips to the food forest. The best time of year to be in the garden generally, despite her access to all the other seasons' incredible produce. The peaches are the moment magic really happens. But it only happens for about a fortnight at most.

Our summer harvest is full of things we preserve for other times – passata, cucumber, pickles, polenta corn and more.

24
JANUARY

Dry. Bone dry. Earth-crackingly dry. For us, this is unusual. We've just come through the driest January in forever. In this particular corner of southern Tasmania, the southernmost shire in the country, dry spells aren't like those where I grew up. My childhood was spent in the sun-kissed mainland Australian interior. Canberra and surrounds aren't blessed with rainfall. Or topsoil. Canberra has a harsher summer, a more punishing winter than Cygnet. But the grasshoppers, the sticky little black flies, the golden-coloured grass that arrive with late summer in Tassie, they're all reminiscent of the hills of my youth. Not that I'm looking at hills.

I skewered my finger this morning. Fifteen millimetres (more than half an inch) of timber has left the firewood I was splitting and inserted itself in the flesh of my hand. It sits, threaded, in the side of my pointer finger, just before the third joint. Half is visible, and the other half lies embedded in my flesh. When I say 'threaded', I'm not kidding. On either end of where this mini wood chip lies, concealed underneath my skin, is visible a few millimetres of wood. I need tweezers. And fast. The pain is excruciating. It's a sign of how weak we humans are, and how weak I am as an individual in particular, that a small fragment of wood can have me incapable of rational thought. My mind is emblazoned with pain. It's all I can do to control my body and stay upright. It's important to pull a splinter like this out, but in which direction? The way the sliver of wood went in, wagering that it is bigger at the top than the bottom? Or the way it was going, so as not to risk a smaller shard of wood shearing off the side of the woodchip and heading off deeper into my flesh?

That, I must say, is all I can think of. Not soil health. Not the yellowing hills and the need for green grass for our dairy cows. Not the need to curb my swearing. I am obsessed with the splinter. And tweezers. WHERE ARE THOSE TWEEZERS?

28
JANUARY

We sit beneath the smoke. Under a Watch and Act alert, the second-highest bushfire warning on the Tasmanian Fire Service website. Just under the Emergency warning. It's the seventh day of smoke. We feel the smoke stinging our eyes, rasping our throats. We watch as charred ferns and bark and leaves rain down from the smudged-out sky. Rarely, we see the sun, red behind the billowing smoke.

And yet, this isn't really our fire. At present it threatens those close to us personally, but a few kilometres removed in reality. Friends with dairy cows, pigs, homes, lives, all hanging in the balance. Day after day, the alerts alter. The radio is alive with news, so much news it becomes as suffocating as the air, but it's news we must have, that we devour, that we obsess over.

Our days are filled with preparations to leave. A bag perpetually packed. Feed for the livestock planned. Decks and grass and the timber cladding of the house soaked. Wallows overflowing. Dams opened to cattle. And always water, water, water, in the paddocks, on the house, pumping it, moving it, spraying it.

In the distance, fire crews, exhausted probably after a month of trying to extinguish blazes – both man-made and from 3000 dry lightning strikes – work incessantly. We see them driving up our road. Patrolling. We see the trucks parked, looking over the Huon River, to where Geeveston and Castle Forbes Bay and Franklin are threatened by a fire so wild that they have to wait for it to appear out of the thick black smoke. We know that they have made so many safe, but that the fires rage in many parts of the state. Dozens of blazes, some destroying ancient Gondwanan forest, others creeping close to rural communities. Tasmania, this year, is gasping for air.

We know that in times like this, we can rely on the fighters of fire. We can rely on our community. We know that this will pass. But we also know that despite living in a rural idyll, fire is a real and present danger. One we hope beyond hope doesn't damage us, our friends, our neighbours, our community, or our incredible natural heritage.

As we watch and wait, life goes on. We must keep those around us, our companions, our children, free from unnecessary worry. We still water the garden, plan harvests, work on menus, even though we have been up every hour during the night to check the horizon and the updates. This is just another thing that life throws at you, not something that defines you. Even now, with uncertainty hanging like the russet haze in the air, we know our lives are more secure than those of so many in the world. So much more certain than many of the vulnerable in our society.

Others bear a far heavier burden in terms of fighting fires and preparing their farms, and being evacuated from their homes. These days will pass soon, though not soon enough.

Busy, busy, busy. Add in winnowing wheat, and there's even less time for the beach.

7 FEBRUARY

The rain falls, building from a few drops to a heavy downpour, like a symphony rising, rising, rising in volume. I feel the rain as though it is dousing my soul, a soothing, drenching, overwhelming force that gives life to the paddocks and death to the fires that have raged over the hill. With it comes relief. The relief of a tragedy averted, a challenge avoided, a threat assuaged.

Summer has burned this year, not just in Tassie's wild places. It has been the hottest anyone has known in these parts, breaking all-time records for days over 30°C, dry days, days over 25°C. Records have tumbled often since we arrived, perhaps because records themselves are a relatively recent import in these climes. Or perhaps records tumble because we haven't had this much carbon dioxide in the atmosphere for a few hundred thousand years. The paddocks have burned off under the baking sun to golden sheaves. Some adolescent trees look parched – even the natives, but more so the imports such as oak and elder. The heat showed perhaps we were unprepared, but this heat, well, it was unexpected.

Weather. It means everything to us, as I've said before. More so at this point in time, when the weather has been kind to us, blowing gently from the east as I write, with more rain, heavy rain, forecast.

The threat to humans and our habitat from bushfires is low and retreating by the day. We are grateful that we, and the people we share our gorgeous valley with, have emerged a little worn but generally unscathed. Healing begins. Blue skies, gentle breezes and low fire risk mean we can draw breath, deep, deep breath, especially when the smoke has almost vanished from our little corner of the state.

Other locals are still unsettled, unnerved, some unhoused. We think of them as we start to live life again as normal. We're glad to get back to the routines, to the humble arts of growing and cooking food in a pretty damn special part of the world.

15
FEBRUARY

We've reached peak zucchini. The garden is bountiful, almost too bountiful, particularly with a few bits and pieces at this time of year, zucchini highest among them. We sliver them finely and put them in salad. We cook them long and hard and make a relish, we ferment them. We chargrill them to serve with fresh pesto. And still there's more than enough for our needs.

I contemplate giving visitors to the farm a few zucchini as a parting gift. These amazing, flavour-packed signs of summer are one that we can't really keep up with in the kitchen. But, as the others on the farm point out, giving someone zucchini, at this time of year, has the potential to be considered an insult.

Gooseberry Sherbet

Serves 4

A sherbet is, in the old-fashioned sense, a dairy dessert that doesn't contain eggs. Think of it like a milk sorbet, or a much smoother version of granita. It's easy for the home cook, because you don't need an ice-cream machine to make a lovely frozen dessert. And it's more refreshing than ice cream, thanks to the lack of eggs and cream. Here, I have used one of my all-time favourite fruits, the gooseberry, which enjoys a very short season indeed.

200 g (7 oz) gooseberries, cleaned

150 g (5½ oz) caster (superfine) sugar, plus extra if needed

250 ml (8½ fl oz/1 cup) full-cream (whole) milk

lemon juice, if needed

strawberries and cream, to serve (optional)

Pop the gooseberries into a small saucepan and place over a low heat to allow them to break down. You want them to stew, but ideally not add any liquid, just use the liquid that comes out of the fruit. Cover, but stir regularly, until the gooseberries are really mushy. Allow to cool enough to handle, then press the fruit through a fine-mesh sieve. Discard the lumpy bits stuck in the sieve and keep the purée underneath.

Warm the sugar with 150 ml (5 fl oz) water in a saucepan over a high heat and stir until the sugar has dissolved. Allow to cool (speed it up by placing the pan's base in cold water), add the gooseberry purée and stir well, then stir in the milk. It could well look curdled, but don't worry about that. Have a taste. Gooseberries vary in sweetness, and you want it to be sweet with a nice acidic tang. Add lemon juice if it's not tangy enough, and a little sugar if it's not sweet enough. Remember though, that when things are frozen you get less flavour and sweetness.

Place this liquid, which is the sherbet base, in a large-ish plastic tray in the freezer (big enough to whisk the sherbet up in later) and freeze for 1 hour. Pull from the freezer and whisk (use a hand whisk) to break up all the ice crystals and redistribute them. Do this every half an hour or hour while the mixture freezes. If you forget it, or your freezer is super efficient and the ice becomes too firm, use a food processor to turn it back into slush. When the mixture is light and airy, allow to freeze for a good hour or longer at the end so it's more like a sorbet than a slushie.

It's delicious alone, but you could serve it with strawberries and cream, too.

Zucchini Tzatziki

Makes 500 g (1 lb 2 oz)

This is a great way to use up leftover roasted or grilled zucchini. A variation on the cucumber-and-yoghurt classic from Greece, this has a bit more body and a nice smoky character.

4 zucchini (courgettes), sliced and roasted or chargrilled

2 tablespoons extra-virgin olive oil

300 g (10½ oz) drained yoghurt (see page 42)

2 garlic cloves, crushed

1 tablespoon chopped fresh mint

2–3 tablespoons chopped fresh dill

1 tablespoon lemon juice

Pulse the zucchini with the olive oil in a food processor until broken down but not completely smooth. Fold into the yoghurt with the garlic, herbs, lemon juice, and salt and pepper to taste.

Serve with Flatbreads (page 306), Ciabatta (page 308), or similar.

Parmesan Grissini

Makes 20 thin grissini

You can use any bread dough, even sourdough if you have it, but the addition of fat and parmesan makes this even better. It's much easier to use a machine to do this, because the fat can make kneading by hand quite messy, as it does with brioche. A tablespoon of finely chopped rosemary leaves, added with the parmesan, is a pretty good thing to add, too.

7 g (¼ oz) sachet active dried yeast

½ teaspoon sugar

250 g (9 oz/1⅔ cups) plain (all-purpose) flour, plus extra for dusting (use a bread [strong] flour if you can find it)

½ teaspoon salt, plus extra salt flakes for sprinkling

170 ml (5½ fl oz/⅔ cup) tepid water (body temperature)

2 tablespoons pork fat

40 g (1½ oz) finely grated parmesan

Combine the yeast, sugar, flour and salt in a large bowl. Make a well in the middle and add the water.

Knead to a dough, smother with the fat, cover and allow to rise in a warm place until doubled in size. Knead again with the parmesan to incorporate all the fat. (A freestanding electric mixer with a dough hook makes this much easier and cleaner, I must say.)

Preheat the oven to 180°C (350°F) and cover a baking sheet with either flour or baking paper.

Cut the dough into 20 even-sized pieces and roll and stretch it out to make rustic-looking strands about 30 cm (12 in) long and thinner than your little finger. Dust with plenty of flour so they don't stick. Lay them out as you go on the tray, and sprinkle with a little more salt at the end if you like. (I occasionally spray them first with a little water to get the salt to stick if the dough is a touch dry.)

I like to bake them pretty quickly after rolling so they are thinner and crisper than if they puff, but it does depend on your taste.

Bake for 15–20 minutes, or until golden brown and reasonably crisp.

Strawberry and Mint Shrub

Makes approx. 400 ml (13½ fl oz)

We often serve a version of this shrub as our welcome drink, a cordial often enhanced with a splash of Tasmanian gin. A shrub isn't just a small tree; it's an old-fashioned thirst quencher that has been making a bit of a comeback. Really, it's like a cordial for grown-ups because it uses vinegar, as well as sugar and fruit, to make an incredibly delicious drink that is fabulous with sparkling water or still, and is very much suited to a mixed drink. It takes a few days to make, so plan ahead.

250 g (9 oz/1⅔ cups) ripe strawberries, hulled and quartered

12 mint leaves

160 g (5½ oz) sugar

200 ml (7 fl oz) good-quality cider vinegar (or white-wine vinegar – the most important part is the quality)

Pop the strawberries, mint and sugar in a non-reactive bowl, stir, cover and set aside on a work surface for 8 hours, or overnight. The sugar should have dissolved to form a syrup by this stage. If the sugar hasn't quite dissolved, stir the mixture until the grains have disappeared. (You can also leave it in the fridge for a few days.)

Add the vinegar to this mix, stir well and leave on the bench in a cool place for 2–3 days. You can actually do this in the fridge and leave it for 2 weeks, but it does take up quite a bit of space. Taste, and the liquid should be intensely strawberry flavoured.

Pass the shrub through a fine-mesh sieve, letting gravity do the work rather than pressing it to speed it up. That's because you want a nice clear liquid, not a purée. Once it has drained well, transfer the shrub (the liquid bit) to a sterilised glass bottle (see Note below) and store in the fridge. It can keep for several months. You can also use the strawberries in a sprightly dessert, rather than discarding them.

Use this syrup to make your drinks. We aim to dilute the shrub with about 3 parts water to 1 part syrup, but let your taste be the guide.

Note on Sterilising

Sterilising jars is important to prevent any unwanted yeasts, moulds or bacteria getting into your preserves. The easiest way at home is to use heat. A jar and lid that have come from a dishwasher are sterile and ready to use. In the absence of a dishwasher, simply place jars and lids in a saucepan filled with cold water so they are submerged. Place on a medium–high heat and bring to the boil. Once they've boiled, they're sterile. Just take care removing from the hot water. (Don't pour boiling water over cold glass, or it will crack.)

Clear Gazpacho with Vodka

Serves 6

Some call it tomato tea, the clear liquid that comes from crushed tomatoes, some, tomato consommé. Here, with a touch of cucumber, there's a bit more going on than straight tomato, so I've called it gazpacho.

1 kg (2 lb 3 oz) very ripe tomatoes (ideally salad ones, not the egg-shaped ones)

1 cucumber, peeled

½ teaspoon salt

120 ml (4 fl oz) vodka, quite chilled

edible flowers, to garnish (optional)

Rub the tomatoes and the cucumber through a grater to break them up well. (Using a food processor is likely to lead to a cloudier result, so I prefer a grater.)

Line a fine-mesh sieve with a clean, disposable cloth or a piece of muslin (cheesecloth) and drain the tomatoes and cucumber into a non-reactive bowl or tub. You're trying to capture the clean, lightly coloured liquid that comes out. Don't press or squeeze it, just let it do its thing. It's easiest to leave it in the fridge overnight, if you've the space.

You can use the solid stuff that's left in the cloth in a soup, or even to thicken a stew, we've found, but for the drink it's the liquid bit you want. Add the salt, or to taste, to the liquid. You want to bring up the tomato character slightly, but not make it taste like soup. Refrigerate until ready to use. When ready, serve in six beakers or glasses, with a tablespoon of vodka in each one. Garnish with edible flowers, if desired.

Roasted Tomatillo Salsa

Makes 1 litre (34 fl oz/4 cups)

This Central American fruit is relatively tasteless until cooked, and it's at its best really cooked until dark. Once that's done, it has a mouth-watering flavour and bracing acidity, which we balance with the sweetness of onion and garlic. We use tomatillo across the seasons, preserved in jars, frozen in tubs and fresh from the garden in summer. This paste is good for eating with corn chips with a bit of chilli, can be paired with Slow-roasted Pork Shoulder (page 198) and provides the base of a heady Pork and Tomatillo Stew (page 258).

1 kg (2 lb 3 oz) tomatillos, papery skin removed

2 onions, skin left on, halved

4 garlic cloves

2 tablespoons dried oregano

1 teaspoon ground cumin

1 teaspoon smoked paprika (optional)

handful of fresh coriander (cilantro), roughly chopped

Preheat the grill (broiler) to high.

Place the tomatillos in a heatproof dish and grill until starting to almost blacken and break down, turning them over if necessary. Remove from the grill and leave to one side.

In another heatproof dish, cook the onion and garlic separately under the grill until the skin starts to darken and the insides are soft. Remove the skins and purée the onion and garlic to a coarse paste in a food processor. Add the tomatillo and pulse until it's fairly broken up, but not smooth. Stir in the oregano, cumin and paprika (if using), and enough salt and pepper to give it some bounce.

Serve as is, topped with the roughly chopped coriander, or with corn chips and jalapeños, in pork tacos, or with roasted pork shoulder.

Eggplant, Dill and Tomato Salad

Serves 6–8

Kind of Turkish, kind of not, it goes best with stronger-flavoured meats like beef or lamb.

- olive oil, for frying
- 10 medium (about 400 g/14 oz) Lebanese eggplants (aubergines), the finger-like ones
- 3 large, ripe tomatoes, chopped into big pieces
- generous pinch of ground cumin (or sumac)
- 2 tablespoons lemon juice
- pinch of sugar (optional)
- 2 tablespoons extra-virgin olive oil
- 4–6 tablespoons chopped dill
- lamb kebabs or leftover roasted beef, to serve

Heat 4 cm (1½ in) oil in a wok over a really high flame. When a breadcrumb dropped into the oil sizzles gently, slide the whole eggplants into the oil and cook, turning regularly, for about 3–4 minutes, or until soft all the way through. Remove with a slotted spoon and drain well. Alternatively, rub the eggplants well with oil and roast in an oven heated to 200°C (400°F) for 15 minutes until tender. Drain well, set aside to cool, then remove the stem and cut the flesh into 2–3 cm (¾–1¼ in) pieces.

Toss the eggplant with the tomato chunks and cumin to taste. Whisk the lemon juice, sugar, oil and dill well and pour over the vegetables. Stir to combine and serve with lamb kebabs or leftover roasted beef.

Stir-fried Eggplant with Sichuan Pepper and Tomato

Serves 6

We like to cook Asian-influenced food at home. This dish, inspired by travels through China, is made all the more delicious by the late addition of garlic and vinegar, a trick I learned from local and Beijing expat Sally Ives, who runs Chinese cooking classes nearby.

- 2 medium eggplants (aubergines), cut into 2 cm (¾ in) dice
- 1 teaspoon salt
- 1 tablespoon Sichuan (flowering) pepper
- 2–3 tablespoons vegetable, olive or peanut oil
- 1 medium tomato, diced
- 1 tablespoon oyster sauce
- 2 garlic cloves, crushed
- 2 tablespoons Chinese black vinegar (Chinkiang vinegar)

Toss the eggplant in a big bowl with the salt and leave to stand for 30 minutes.

In the meantime, dry-roast the Sichuan pepper in a small frying pan over a low heat until toasty but not burnt.

When ready to cook, drain the eggplant and pat dry with paper towel. Heat 2 tablespoons of the oil in a very hot wok over an insanely high flame and fry the eggplant, tossing or stirring regularly, until it starts to brown a little on most sides. Add a touch more oil if needed.

When the eggplant is the right colour, toss in the pepper and stir for 30 seconds. Add the tomato and oyster sauce and toss again. Remove from the heat and throw in the garlic and vinegar. Stir to combine, tip into a serving dish and eat immediately with lots of rice and some other dishes, Chinese style.

Cucumber, Coriander Flowers and Kunzea

Serves 6

We like doing simple salads using fresh cucumbers, as they cool us down and taste so refreshing. Kunzea is a native Tasmania herb, which has a little citrusy tang and fresh herbaceous note. In its absence, you can use a little lemon zest, or some freshly chopped lemon thyme. As gardeners, we often switch things around, so if there are no coriander flowers but there are the fresh green seeds that come after flowering, we might use a scattering of them with cucumbers instead.

2 telegraph (long) cucumbers, peeled if thick-skinned

juice of 1 lemon

½ teaspoon dried and ground kunzea leaves

a good few pinches of salt

10 coriander (cilantro) flowers

Cut the cucumbers into bite-sized chunks. Toss with the lemon and kunzea leaves, and leave to stand for 10 minutes.

When ready to serve, toss with the salt, some freshly ground black pepper and the coriander flowers, and serve immediately.

Slow-roasted Pork Shoulder

Serves 12

We use this style of pork in our shredded pork buns, for feasts with tomatillo, or over roasted potatoes with mustard. The simplicity of the recipe means it is totally reliant on good ingredients: old-breed, free-range pork, pungent rosemary and Australian garlic.

2 kg (4 lb 6 oz) pork shoulder, ideally skin on

50 g (1¾ oz) fine salt

2 rosemary stalks

8 garlic cloves, peeled

3 tablespoons fennel seeds

It's pretty important to cure the meat overnight, or two nights is even better. Take the pork and place it in a non-reactive tray (glass or plastic will work). Make sure it's meat side up. Sprinkle the salt evenly over all the non-skin surfaces. The reason we do this is because the meat cures faster than the skin when seasoned. Turn so that the skin side is up. Cover and refrigerate overnight.

The next day, preheat the oven to 130°C (265°F). We cook it in a wood oven overnight at about 110°C (230°F) or thereabouts, but a conventional oven can do a pretty good job, too.

Get a roasting tin that is just about the same size as the piece of shoulder. Lay the rosemary and garlic cloves in the base of the tin. Take the meat from the tub or tray it was cured in, drain off any juices, and sprinkle the meaty side with the fennel seeds, including inside any cut bits. Lay it meat side down, skin side up, in the tin and roast slowly in the oven for about 3–4 hours, or until it falls apart when pressed.

Remove from the oven and, when cool enough to handle, remove the skin (you can try crisping it in the oven, but it's very much poor man's crackling). Remove any gristly bits or blood vessels from the meat (shoulders usually have a couple), and gently pull the rest into chunks.

Reheat the oven, this time to 180°C (350°F). Return the pork to the oven with all its fat and juices to lightly brown the top, stirring twice. Check for salt and serve when tickety-boo.

Goat Shoulder Moussaka

Serves 10–12

You can use lamb or goat meat in this, a lovely take on the Greek classic. If you want to use a bit less meat, it's nice to use sliced potato in place of some of the meat – just add it for the final cooking stage. If you're going to make moussaka, bake a big one like this for leftovers another day.

125 ml (4 fl oz/½ cup) olive oil, plus 3–4 tablespoons extra

2 kg (4 lb 6 oz) goat or lamb shoulder meat, diced

2 onions, diced

6 garlic cloves, crushed

250 g (9 oz/1 cup) tomato passata (puréed tomatoes)

bunch of oregano

bunch of thyme

100 ml (3½ fl oz) white wine

1 tablespoon ground cinnamon

4 large eggplants (aubergines), sliced 2 cm (¾ in) thick

750 g (1 lb 11 oz/3 cups) ricotta

200 g (7 oz) kefalograviera cheese (available at Greek delis), grated or crumbled

2 free-range eggs

Greek salad, to serve

Heat 2 tablespoons of the oil in a large, heavy-based saucepan over a whopping heat and sear the goat in three batches, turning regularly until evenly browned. Add more oil when necessary and be sure to rub the base of the pan with a wooden spoon to get any of the stuck-on bits (the yummy bits) before they burn. Transfer the goat to a bowl as you go.

Once all the meat is browned, turn down the heat to medium–high, add the onion to the pan and cook for 3–4 minutes, or until starting to soften and colour. (Again, you may need to sneak in a touch more olive oil if there's not enough to fry it nicely.) Add the garlic and cook for a further minute, then stir in the tomato passata. Cook, stirring occasionally, for a further 2 minutes, or until the tomato is slightly coloured.

Preheat the oven to 150°C (300°F).

Wrap the herbs in a piece of muslin (cheesecloth) and tie with twine. (Alternatively, simply add the bunches as they are and pick out after cooking.) Add the herbs to the pan with the wine, cinnamon and 500 ml (17 fl oz/2 cups) water. Bring to the boil, then return the goat to the pan and cover with a tight-fitting lid. Bake for 2 hours, or until tender. Season with salt and pepper, and roughly shred the meat.

Meanwhile, soak the eggplant in water for 1 hour. Drain, then pat dry with paper towel. Heat the 125 ml (4 fl oz/½ cup) oil in a large frying pan over a medium heat. Cook the eggplant in batches, for 3 minutes each side, or until golden. Transfer to a tray lined with paper towel.

Reheat the oven to 180°C (350°F).

In a big bowl, mix the ricotta, kefalograviera and eggs really well to combine. When the goat is cooked, place a layer of eggplant (about one-third of the total) in the base of a 3 litre (101 fl oz/12 cup) ovenproof dish, then spread half the goat on top. Add another layer of eggplant, then the remaining goat. Top with the remaining eggplant and spread over the ricotta mixture.

Bake the moussaka for 50 minutes, or until the top is golden brown. Serve with a Greek salad.

Vegetarian Moussaka

Serves 6

While I do love a bit of lamb or goat in my moussaka, this version, with potato along with the obligatory eggplant, is a lovely take on the original. If your ricotta is a bit dry, add a splash of milk or cream to loosen it up a bit.

6 large eggplants (aubergines), sliced 1 cm (½ in) thick

150 ml (5 fl oz) extra-virgin olive oil

2 onions, diced

6 garlic cloves, crushed

400 ml (13½ fl oz) tinned crushed tomatoes

2 tablespoons good-quality dried oregano

1 tablespoon fresh thyme leaves

1 teaspoon ground cinnamon

375 g (13 oz/1½ cups) ricotta

100 g (3½ oz) kefalograviera cheese (available at Greek delis)

2 free-range eggs

4 large potatoes (about 600 g/1 lb 5 oz), sliced 5 mm (¼ in) thick

Zucchini Tzatziki (page 189) and Greek salad, to serve

Soak the eggplant in water for 1 hour. Drain, then pat dry with paper towel. Heat 125 ml (4 fl oz/½ cup) of the oil in a large frying pan over a medium heat. Cook the eggplant, in batches, for 3 minutes each side, or until golden. Transfer to a tray lined with paper towel.

Heat the remaining oil in a large, heavy-based saucepan over a medium heat and fry the onions for 5–6 minutes, or until soft and starting to brown. Add the garlic and cook for a further 1 minute, then stir in 3 tablespoons of the chopped tomato, the oregano, thyme and cinnamon. Cook, stirring occasionally, for a further 5 or so minutes, or until slightly coloured. (This gentle drying out of the tomato and browning gives great depth of flavour to the finished dish. It's not essential, but nice to do.) Add the rest of the tomato and about 100 ml (3½ fl oz) water, depending on the texture of your sauce. Bring back to the boil, simmer for 5 minutes, then season with salt and pepper.

Preheat the oven to 170°C (340°F).

Combine the cheeses with the eggs in a bowl. When the sauce is ready, place a layer of eggplant in the base of a 3 litre (101 fl oz/12 cup) ovenproof dish, then lay the sliced potato on top and spread half the tomato on top of that. Add another layer of eggplant and the remaining tomato. Spread over the ricotta mixture, though depending on texture I sometimes blob it on.

Bake the moussaka for 40–50 minutes, or until the top is golden brown and the potato is cooked. Serve with the tzatziki and a Greek salad.

Heirloom Tomato, Padrón and Goat's Curd Salad

Serves 6

The padrón pepper is a Spanish chilli, which, through some quirk, is only hot about 10–20 per cent of the time. So, mostly, it's a mild sparkle of heat in the chilli, with the Russian roulette of extra-hot spice occasionally there to keep you on your feet. Served simply fried and with lemon juice as a bar snack, the padrón's flavour also goes amazingly well with other summer harvests – tomatoes, basil and a lively goat's curd.

100 g (3½ oz) goat's curd

6 large tomatoes, sliced or cut into wedges, depending on the size (a few varieties make for a more interesting meal)

6 basil leaves, torn

3 tablespoons extra-virgin olive oil

6 padrón peppers, fried or roasted

crusty bread, to serve

Dollop a big spoonful of goat's cheese on a platter, or on plates. Lay the sliced tomato over the curd neatly. Sprinkle the tomato with salt and pepper, then dot the basil around, drizzle with the oil and leave to stand for 10 minutes.

To serve, lay the padrón over the tomatoes and offer some good crusty bread.

Tomatoes

I'll let you in on a little gardener's secret. The best tomatoes aren't 'vine-ripened'. Well, they might be, but not in most places in summer. That's because the best-tasting tomatoes are ripened below 25°C. Above that and they risk going floury. So all those tomatoes sold as 'vine ripened'? They might just be left on the stem, but still gassed using ethylene after being harvested green. As gardeners, we pick them after they've coloured up, but before they start to soften too much, and let them ripen on the kitchen bench.

Now, tomatoes, up until peak ripeness, also shouldn't be stored in the fridge. A few days in the fridge and you'll never get the same flavour from those tomatoes again. The magic taste dissipates in cold storage.

Tomatoes are one of our staples. We use them prolifically in the season, simply fresh and sweet and matched with goat's curd or the like. And out of season we draw on litres of passata that we put up just in case. In case we want a stew, or a pizza, or a pasta, or anything else that needs a little lovely tomato flavour.

We use a greenhouse to get some early season tomatoes, but unlike eggplant and capsicum, which don't ripen in our temperate, maritime climate (43 degrees south and surrounded by water), we can ripen tomatoes outdoors. Mostly, if they're outside, they're an autumn crop.

Here are a few of our favourite tomatoes (you might find that in lower latitudes you'll get different varieties to our fast-ripening cool-climate ones).

Wapsipinicon Peach

A glorious sweet tomato with yellow flesh and a slightly fuzzy feel, like a peach. Sometimes they even get a little blush like a peach on the skin. These are smallish in size, and great in salads or fresh. Arguably our favourite eating tomato.

Jaune Flamme

Meaning yellow flame, this French variety is full of juice, so it's terrible for cooking, but amazing for flavour in a fresh tomato salad or the like. Interestingly, the colour is way more orange than it is yellow.

Azoychka

A Russian early ripener, yellow, large and fleshy. A good all rounder of the beefsteak type.

Ananas Noire

Meaning 'black pineapple' in French, these can be anything from yellow to green to black to red. Ribbed in shape, with amazing depth of flavour, we're always excited to see these in the mix.

San Marzano

The archetypal Neapolitan saucing tomato, this makes the best passata, and hence also the most amazing pasta sauce. It's one of what is known as the roma or egg tomato type, which have more flesh to jelly ratio and are best for preserving.

Green Zebra

A cracking salad-style tomato with decent acid, a great fragrance and a striking look.

Broad Ripple Yellow Currant

Well, you know how I said the best-tasting tomatoes aren't ripened on the vine? I lied. These sweet bliss balls, the size of marbles, are best straight from the highly productive plant. They often rip a little when pulled from the stem, so are best eaten within hours of picking. We think of them as gardeners' tomatoes, because most are eaten as a snack while working in the garden.

FAT PIG
FARM

Fermented Cucumbers

Makes 500 g (1 lb 2 oz)

You can make pickled cucumbers using vinegar and salt, and perhaps even some sugar, but fermenting them adds a whole new layer of complexity. We add vine leaves or tea leaves to the mix to help stop them going too soft. Try this with zucchini, too, in the peak of the season if you're running out of ways to use them.

500 g (1 lb 2 oz) small pickling cucumbers

30 g (1 oz) salt

1 grape vine leaf, well washed (or use ¼ teaspoon black tea leaves)

1 teaspoon dill seeds (optional)

Scrub the cucumbers well and, if they're tiny, use them whole. If they are bigger, cut them into chunks about 3 cm (1¼ in) long and about 1 cm (½ in) or so wide, making sure each piece has skin attached.

Place the cucumbers in a large, sterilised (see Note on page 192) sealable pickling jar (glass is great because it doesn't react), or in two or three jars if that's all you've got. Make sure they're wide-mouthed jars, and leave room at the top for the liquid.

Heat 500 ml (17 fl oz/2 cups) water, the salt and vine leaf in a saucepan over a moderate heat, whisking just until the salt has dissolved. Spoon the dill seeds over, if using, and when the water has cooled enough so you can hold the pan with your hand, pour the pickling liquid over the cucumbers until they are well covered. You can weigh them down with a smaller jar if necessary so the cucumber is under the liquid. Cover with a clean cloth so that insects can't get in but air can, and leave in a warm but not sunny place for a few days to ferment. It can start to fizz in a day or two, but will take about a week to fully ferment. Taste it every day to see how it's going, because once it's reached the flavour you want, it's important to get it into the fridge.

Once the cucumbers reach the desired flavour (a bit sour, with a salty tang, and some subtle funkiness along with the sweetness of the original fruit), cover tightly with the lid and place in the fridge. They are still a fresh product, and are best consumed within a month.

Use with salami, in sandwiches with pastrami or cheese, or use in a goulash.

Garlic-fried Green Beans

Serves 2

This recipe, based on a Chinese-style stir-fry, uses a bit of pork to flavour the beans, though you can ditch the pork in favour of a shiitake mushroom or two. It's a side dish, but can be served as a quick dinner with rice and some fermented chilli paste or the like.

2 tablespoons pork fat or olive oil, plus extra if needed

2 tablespoons minced (ground) pork

300 g (10½ oz) green beans, topped and tailed, halved if long

2 garlic cloves, roughly chopped

1 tablespoon cider vinegar

Heat the fat in a very hot wok or heavy-based frying pan over a raging, roaring flame.

Add the mince and break it up with a wooden spoon as you quickly stir-fry and brown it. Once cooked, remove the meat with a slotted spoon and set aside. In the same wok or pan, over a similarly scorching heat, fry the beans, adding a touch more pork fat if needed. Toss the beans regularly so they brown a bit as they cook, for about 2 minutes, seasoning with salt and pepper as you go. Add the meat back to the wok, stir once, then remove from the heat and stir in the garlic. Give it just a few seconds as you stir, then add the vinegar and toss to coat. The pan should still be hot enough at this stage to just quickly cook the vinegar. Taste for seasoning, and serve immediately.

Home-made Digestives (Oatmeal Biscuits)

Makes approx. 20 biscuits

I'm a big fan of gorgeous home-made biscuits, and these semi-sweet oat biscuits are perfect for soft cheese.

200 g (7 oz/1⅓ cups) plain (all-purpose) flour, plus extra for dusting

1 teaspoon salt

50 g (1¾ oz/½ cup) rolled oats (try quick-cook oats for a finer result)

50 g (1¾ oz) caster (superfine) sugar

1 teaspoon baking powder

100 g (3½ oz) chilled, diced butter or chilled lard, or a mixture

2 tablespoons full-cream (whole) milk, for mixing

Preheat the oven to 200°C (400°F).

Mix the dry ingredients together in a big bowl and rub the butter in thoroughly with your fingertips. You can also do this by pulsing the ingredients in a food processor. Mix in the milk to give a firm dough. Turn onto a floured board, knead lightly for 2 minutes, adding more flour if it gets sticky.

Roll the dough out rather thinly, about 3–4 mm (⅛ in), then cut into 7 cm (2¾ in) rounds. Place the biscuits on a baking tray lined with baking paper, prick them well and bake until they turn a light tan colour, about 15 minutes. (If using lard, the biscuits will have a paler colour.) Cool and store in an airtight container for up to 2 weeks.

Serve spread with a soft, fresh cheese, perhaps some new-season goat's cheese or a squidgy white mould cheese such as brie.

Caramelised Saffron Peaches with Raspberries and Vanilla Honey Mascarpone

Serves 4

Rain on a hot tin roof. The smell of salt in the air and the hair. The intoxicating perfume of peaches. Raspberries, raspberries, raspberries. These are the scents of summer.

250 g (9 oz) sugar

generous pinch of saffron

few blades of mace

4 large, ripe peaches, peeled, quartered and stoned

200 g (7 oz) Home-made Mascarpone (page 312)

1 vanilla bean, seeds scraped (or 1 teaspoon vanilla extract)

2 tablespoons fragrant honey

caster (superfine) sugar, for dusting

2–3 tablespoons butter, for frying

150 g (5½ oz) fresh raspberries

Combine the sugar, saffron and mace with 500 ml (17 fl oz/ 2 cups) water in a saucepan and simmer for 10 minutes. Add the peaches, bring back to the boil and turn off the heat. Allow the peaches to cool in this liquid. (Do this a couple of days ahead and they will taste even better.)

Stir the mascarpone gently with the vanilla seeds and honey.

When ready to eat, drain the peaches well (reserve the syrup for your next batch of fruit) and roll in the caster sugar. Heat the butter in a non-stick frying pan and fry the peach quarters over a medium heat to caramelise. Serve with the raspberries and a drool of mascarpone.

Strawberries and Rose Cream

Serves 4

How good is this? Serve and see. If you don't have them in the garden, buy ripe strawberries from the coolest region you can find, for a more intense flavour. In the past, I have infused my cream with four crushed leaves of rose geranium, but rosewater is a good substitute.

300 ml (10 fl oz) pouring (single/light) cream

1–2 teaspoons rosewater

3–4 tablespoons caster (superfine) sugar, to taste

750 g (1 lb 11 oz/5 cups) strawberries, hulled and halved if large

Tip the cream into a big mixing bowl and whisk in the rosewater and sugar until it just begins to thicken. Add the strawberries and gently crush a few with your spoon as you fold them in.

I like to make it half an hour before serving to allow the flavours to meld, but knock it out straight away if you want.

Serve with a glass of something good, even a sweet Champagne.

Welsh Cakes

Makes about 10 individual cakes

These aren't so much cakes as gently fried, scone-like batter discs that are very light, with a crisp outside. You can serve them with butter and/or honey or jam, but when they're fresh, they're lovely as is. I cook mine on a Welsh bakestone, forged at Coegnant Colliery in 1932. It was a wedding present from the local blacksmith to Dorothy and Edgar Evans, whose grandson, Peter (no relation), gifted it to me. It is quite prized in our household, but a decent heavy-based frying pan works well too.

240 g (8½ oz) self-raising flour, plus extra for dusting

90 g (3 oz) caster (superfine) sugar

120 g (4½ oz) butter, chilled and diced

1 free-range egg, lightly beaten

100 g (3½ oz/⅔ cup) currants, sultanas, mixed peel

1 tablespoon full-cream (whole) milk

2–3 tablespoons vegetable oil and butter, for frying

Rub the flour, sugar and butter together until the mixture resembles breadcrumbs. Add the egg and gently combine. Add the currant mix and milk and form into a ball.

Roll out the dough on a floured bench to about 1 cm (½ in) thick and cut into 3 cm (1¼ in) rounds with a cutter (some people use a fluted cutter).

Heat the vegetable oil and butter in a frying pan over a medium-low heat. Fry the Welsh cakes until browned on one side, then turn gently and fry the other side. Take care that they cook in the middle – about 3–4 minutes each side should do it. Allow to cool a bit before serving. Welsh cakes are at their best just cooked, but the next day they're good with cream.

Marshmallow Meringue with Strawberries and Rose Cream, Rhubarb and Early Basil

Serves 6

We do love mayonnaise. So what has that got to do with this? Well, if you use the egg yolks for mayo, you've got egg whites ready for meringue! It doesn't need much, just a garnish of fruit, and if you make your own mascarpone (see page 312), it's the business. Here, we've used the delicate flavour of strawberries and rosewater, our own fragrant green rhubarb and some fino verde basil, an early season basil that has a touch of spice and grows well in a pot.

3 free-range eggs, separated

80 g (2¾ oz/⅓ cup) caster (superfine) sugar

½ teaspoon white-wine vinegar

1 teaspoon cornflour (cornstarch)

a few drops of vanilla extract

Strawberries and Rose Cream (page 211), or Home-made Mascarpone (page 312), to serve

poached rhubarb, to serve

fino verde basil, to serve

Preheat the oven to 140°C (275°F).

Beat the egg whites until soft peaks form, then whisk in the sugar, followed by the vinegar, cornflour and vanilla.

Spread into a 20 cm (8 in) round on a lined baking tray using a spatula to give it vertical sides and a flattish top. Don't be pedantic about it. Bake for 10 minutes, then reduce the oven temperature to 120°C (250°F) for about 1½ hours, checking that it doesn't brown overly much. Turn the oven off, open the door slightly and leave the meringue inside until cool.

Serve with strawberries and rose cream, poached rhubarb and basil. Fresh berries and home-made mascarpone are cracking accompaniments, too.

Honey and Orange Blossom Marshmallows

Makes approx. 50

Making marshmallows at home is really easy, so long as you follow some rules. Temperature and timing are vitally important, so it's ideal if you have a cooking thermometer, though you could try to wing it and just guess the temperature. An electric mixer will save your arm from getting sore, too, though at the end you can whisk over a bowl of ice to speed up the cooling process. I used a Middle Eastern brand of orange-blossom water. Some are stronger than others, so perhaps only use half and taste the mixture just before you finish whisking and add more to taste if needed.

30 g (1 oz) honey

250 g (9 oz) caster (superfine) sugar

3 tablespoons powdered gelatine

3 free-range egg whites

pinch of salt

2 teaspoons lemon juice

finely grated zest of ¼ lemon (about 1 teaspoon)

½ teaspoon vanilla extract

1–2 teaspoons orange-blossom water

60 g (2 oz/½ cup) icing mixture, for dusting (see Note)

You're going to be doing three things at once, so try to keep an eye on everything as you go. Heat the honey with the sugar and 2 tablespoons water in small pan, stirring to dissolve the sugar every now and then, until the mixture reaches 118°C (244°F) on a cooking thermometer.

While the honey mixture heats, dissolve the gelatine in 80 ml (2½ fl oz/⅓ cup) water in a small, heatproof bowl set over a small saucepan of simmering water until warm and runny.

When the sugar and gelatine are nearly ready, start to whisk the egg whites with the salt, lemon juice and zest, and the vanilla and orange-blossom water in a freestanding electric mixer. Keep whisking until firm peaks form. When the peaks form, you want to whisk in the hot honey mixture in a thin stream and keep whisking while you pour in the hot, runny gelatine mixture. Continue whisking until the bowl is just slightly warmer than your hand to the touch. This will probably take more than another 10 minutes – I allow 15.

When barely still warm, spread the marshmallow mixture out on a lined 20 cm (8 in) square or similar ovenproof dish to at least 2 cm (¾ in) deep. Allow to set completely at room temperature (give it several hours), then dust the top with icing mixture. Cut (use a well-dusted knife or scissors dipped in icing mixture between cuts) and dust with more icing mixture all over. Scorch with a blowtorch if you like, and serve with hot chocolate or just on their own.

Note

Icing mixture differs from straight icing (confectioners') sugar in that it contains a small amount of cornflour (cornstarch). Icing sugar will dissolve too quickly, hence the use of icing mixture for most things where a dusting is required.

The Market Garden

Maybe we misnamed the farm. Once, when all we did was markets and we mostly sold pork, the name Fat Pig Farm was a funny way to recognise that slow-grown, free-ranging old-breed pigs, those that aren't fed a bunch of pharmaceuticals, boast that all-important, flavoursome fat. But in reality, our pigs only take up a tiny percentage of the farm, and Sadie thinks we should be called Fat Cow Farm because they get the run of it more than pigs. Or even more so, Fat Turnip Farm because the garden is such a powerhouse.

We have 70 garden beds, averaging 15 metres long, used to grow our annual crops. That's 1 kilometre worth of mounded beds, all tended using organic principles, and all tended by hand. Once the beds are formed, unless we're growing spuds, the ground is left unturned, the soil left undisturbed so the life within it is unharmed.

We also have perennial crops, things that aren't sown and harvested each year, but live on from year to year. There are three rows of raspberries. There's a mini food forest, with apricots, quince, peach, nectarine and nut trees. We have planted an olive grove, which has just now produced the first fledgling crop after two and a bit years in the ground. There are chestnuts and almonds, sour cherries, damsons, medlars, and pears. We grow elder trees, eager for umbels and umbels of elderflowers in seasons to come, and we have planted sloes, whose dark berries will one day scent our gin. The garden, so much of it, is in its infancy, but produce it does.

To me, the garden is a magical space. I look after the 68 acres that aren't garden, and this patch is managed by others. Jonathan Cooper took the area from overrun paddock and a small house garden to a cranking, glorious commercial market garden. For two years we've worked with Nadia Danti, a woman grown from generations of gardeners, who tended the soil with such care we were humbled, and overwhelmed, with the harvest. And it's now Sadie, my partner in farming and life, who tends the garden. If I venture in, I am but a labourer. It's a magic garden because stuff just grows and grows and the kitchen is utterly blessed with produce not only straight from the ground, but produce that tastes of its place and of itself.

There are estimates that conventionally grown produce in Australia has half the nutrient density that it had 80 years ago. As a nation, we're growing nutritionally poorer foods, to feed a population that's even less likely to eat fresh fruit and veg than their great-grandparents. Why has the nutrient content dropped? (And we're talking micronutrients here, not macronutrients such as protein, carbohydrate etc.) It's because of the way food is usually grown.

On Fat Pig Farm, we obsess over soil health. The more microbes and fungi and nematodes in the soil, the better. It's these that provide what a plant wants. In a miracle of chemistry, plants capture the energy from sunlight, using photosynthesis, to turn carbon dioxide into carbohydrate, i.e. sugars. And these sugars are useful to us, but also to those billions of bacteria and protozoa under the soil that actually feed the plants.

Plants don't eat dirt. They get the nutrients they need and want from the action of microbes. And the way that works is that the microbes need the same things all living things do: air, water, food and the right temperature. We water the garden and try not to compact the beds so they get enough air, occasionally opening up cracks in the soil with a broad fork. And the food for the microbes, the living things in soil? Well, they swap nutrients the plants need for sugars the plants have transformed from the air. It's this whole underground economy. Some plants give up to 80 per cent of the carbohydrate they produce to the microbes that feed their roots.

So the more microbes you can have in soil, in terms of absolute numbers and their variety, the more a plant can access a kaleidoscope of micronutrients. This is great for plant health and vitality. Now, there's also great evidence that a varied diet, with a wide variety of micronutrients, is exactly what humans have evolved to eat. It's good for our resilience, too, and good for our microbiome, the billions of bacteria that inhabit our bodies as well.

From a cook's perspective, the beautiful synergy goes even further. That's because the more nutrient dense a food is, the better it tastes. It seems we are all somehow gifted with this amazing ability to tell the nutrient load of food. If an ingredient seems more complex, more delicious, more nuanced, it has more goodness built in. Flavour is an indicator of nutrient density, and all we have to do is eat, and get more pleasure, from properly grown food. Elegant heh?

So the reason we obsess about soil is not only about the long-term health of the farm and its productivity. It's also about the pleasure of good food, shared at the table, and the ability to spread joy through the act of cooking, and serving, the bounty of what grows in our market garden.

Duck Egg Lemon Shortcakes with Strawberries and Elderflower Cream

Makes 24 little cakes

We sometimes eat dessert as a snack on Christmas Day, rather than just after the meal. Shortbreads, mince pies, gingerbreads, spice biscuits: they all get a guernsey if not on the day, then in the weeks leading up to the big day. These shortcakes, which came to us from our good mate Michelle Crawford, are a new addition to the mix, though they're really nice in a bowl full of strawberries and cream, too.

100 g (3½ oz) butter, softened, plus extra for greasing

100 g (3½ oz) caster (superfine) sugar, plus extra for dusting

2 duck eggs (chook eggs are fine if you can't get duck eggs)

½ teaspoon vanilla extract

generous pinch of salt

finely grated zest of 1 large lemon

200 g (7 oz/about 1⅓ cups) plain (all-purpose) flour

⅛ teaspoon baking powder

150 ml (5 fl oz) pouring (single/light) cream

2 teaspoons elderflower cordial or concentrate

2 teaspoons icing (confectioners') sugar

2 punnets strawberries, hulled and cut into strips or quarters

Preheat the oven to 180°C (350°F).

Grease and lightly sugar 24 gem scones (two trays) or two 12-hole mini muffin trays.

Cream the butter and sugar well until very pale and creamy-looking. Beat in the eggs, one at a time, until soft and light, then beat in the vanilla, salt and lemon zest.

Fold in the flour and baking powder until just combined. Spoon this mixture into the prepared trays, leaving a little room at the top for expansion. It's neater if you flatten the top, but I don't.

Bake in the centre of the oven for about 10–12 minutes, or until starting to brown and a skewer inserted in the middle of a cake comes out clean. Remove from the oven and cool for 10 minutes, then remove from the trays.

Whip the cream with the elderflower and icing sugar. Dress each shortcake with cream and top with a piece of strawberry or three.

Roasted Yellow Nectarines with Orange-Blossom Water and Ginger Crumbs

Serves 4

There's often no need to do much with good stone fruit. But in the peak of the season, or if you have picked the fruit just a tad too early, another option is to cook it. Here, then, is a simple idea to make good on the glut.

4 ripe yellow nectarines, blanched, peeled, halved and stones removed

2 tablespoons sugar

1 teaspoon orange-blossom water

3 ginger nut biscuits, pounded into crumbs (or use plain biscuits mixed with ½ teaspoon ground ginger)

Preheat the oven (or grill) to 250°C (480°F).

Lay the nectarines, cut side down, on a flat, ovenproof serving dish lined with baking paper, then sprinkle with the sugar. Bake for 5 minutes, or until tender.

Sprinkle with the blossom water and crumbs and grill or bake for a few more minutes just to darken the crumbs slightly.

Peach and Lemon Syrup Cake with Gin

Serves 8–10

I adore lemon and lime with gin, hence any excuse to knock up this cake. If it's going to be eaten by the kids, use a few juniper berries in the syrup instead of the gin – just strain them out before using on the cake.

125 g (4½ oz/½ cup) butter, softened, plus extra for greasing

200 g (7 oz) caster (superfine) sugar

3 free-range eggs

finely grated zest of 1 lime, and juice of ½ lime

juice and finely grated zest of ½ lemon

200 g (7 oz/1⅓ cups) self-raising flour

50 g (1¾ oz) almond meal (ground almonds)

200 g (7 oz) plain yoghurt

2 medium peaches, peeled (ideally) and cut into wedges

150 g (5½ oz) sugar

2 tablespoons gin

2 tablespoons raw (demerara) sugar

whipped or runny cream, to serve

Preheat the oven to 180°C (350°F). Grease and line a 20 cm (8 in) round cake tin.

Cream the butter and caster sugar until pale and light. Beat in the eggs, one at a time. Fold in the zests, flour and almond meal gently, then fold in the yoghurt. Use a spatula to scrape the mix into the prepared cake tin, making a small dip in the centre of the cake mixture so that it rises more evenly. Top with the chunks of peach.

Bake for 30–40 minutes, or until a skewer inserted in the middle of the cake comes out clean.

While the cake cooks, heat 60 ml (2 fl oz/¼ cup) water with the sugar and the lime and lemon juice in a small saucepan. Simmer for 5 minutes. When the cake is cooked, take it out of the oven and poke the surface about 30 times with a fine skewer. Quickly reheat the lemon syrup, add the gin, and spoon over the cake. Try to spoon it so that it soaks into the holes evenly rather than all soaking into the edges around the tin.

Sprinkle with raw sugar while the top is still wet. Allow the cake to cool in the tin before removing. Serve with lightly whipped cream or a little runny cream.

Strawberry and Rhubarb Tartlets

Makes 6

Strawberries and rhubarb make excellent bedfellows, and here they're combined with home-made pastry and a little rich custard in tarts.

1 small bunch rhubarb

80 g (2¾ oz/⅓ cup) brown sugar

500 g (1 lb 2 oz) strawberries

4 free-range egg yolks

100 g (3½ oz) caster (superfine) sugar

300 ml (10 fl oz) pouring (single/light) cream

icing (confectioners') sugar and a blow-torch, for glazing

clotted cream, to serve

Pastry

200 g (7 oz/1⅓ cups) plain (all-purpose) flour, plus extra for dusting

120 g (4½ oz) butter, chilled and diced

1 tablespoon caster (superfine) sugar

1 free-range egg yolk

1 tablespoon iced water

To make the pastry, blend the flour, butter and sugar in a food processor until just combined and the mixture looks like breadcrumbs. Pulse in the egg yolk and enough iced water to combine. Tip onto a clean bench and press together to make a ball. Wrap tightly in plastic wrap and pop into the fridge to rest for 30 minutes.

Preheat the oven to 180°C (350°F).

Roll out on a well-floured board to line six 10 cm (4 in) tart tins (you may have to gather and re-roll the pastry to line all six tins). Rest, covered, in the fridge for a further 30 minutes (if you've the time), then blind-bake (see Note on page 109). Just be careful not to brown the pastry. Leave to cool slightly. When ready to cook, reheat the oven to 180°C (350°F).

Wash the rhubarb and cut into 2 cm (¾ in) lengths. Place in a single layer, close together, on a baking tray lined with baking paper and sprinkle with the brown sugar. Bake for about 15 minutes, or until soft, then remove from the oven.

Cut the strawberries into bite-sized pieces and plonk in the pastry cases. Put some rhubarb in with them and lay out the tins on two baking trays. Whisk the egg yolk, caster sugar and cream until smooth and pour very gingerly around the fruit in the tart cases. Fill, but don't overfill, as any spillage can make getting the tartlets out of the tins a little hard. Bake for about 15–20 minutes, or until the custard has set.

To glaze, generously dust the tartlets with icing sugar and use a blowtorch to scorch the top. Alternatively, you can put them under a hot grill (broiler) to melt the icing sugar, or just dust with a bit of icing sugar for looks and not glaze them at all.

Allow the tartlets to cool in the tins before removing and eating the same day with clotted cream.

Appletini

Serves 1 (it's potent!)

We were taught to make this drink by our good friend Natalie Fryar from Abel Gin. We 'fat wash' the spirit for this lovely apple cocktail with aged prosciutto, by dunking slivers of the prosciutto in it prior to mixing. This isn't essential, but it does make for a far better drink, something way beyond your usual cocktail, giving it a different aroma and mouthfeel. If you can't get apple spirit, you can do something similar using calvados or a good spirit such as vodka, though you may want to play with the quantities of apple juice and the like to get the perfect flavour.

45 ml (1½ fl oz) apple spirit

1 small sliver fatty prosciutto or similar (only use naturally cured meats, and something unsmoked)

45 ml (1½ fl oz) apple juice

150 ml (5 fl oz) sparkling water

1 slice dried apple crisp, to serve (optional)

1 slice crispy prosciutto, to serve (optional)

Put the spirit into a small beaker or jar. Plop the fatty prosciutto into the spirit and swirl it around to extract the fragrance. It'll take about 2 minutes.

In a serving glass, place the apple juice and sparkling water. Add the spirit, minus the piece of fatty prosciutto (we actually use this drunken prosciutto as a snack, too!). Top with the dried apple, and serve with the crispy prosciutto lain across the top of the glass.

Note

To crisp the prosciutto, preheat the oven to 130°C (265°F), lay the prosciutto on a lined baking tray, cover with another sheet of baking paper, and top with a second tray to hold it flat while it cooks. Bake for about 15 minutes, or until it has rendered and is starting to colour. Remove the top tray and finish cooking until is a nice even brown, but not too coloured – just 5 minutes probably.

The apple harvest starts in earnest, just as the summer heat wanes and the seasons turn.

Autumn

Apples, pears and quinces
The first frost
Wild mushrooms
Greening paddocks
Rainbows
Golden light
Leaves turning
Dew
Goulash
Chestnuts
Acorns to pigs
Salami making
Flame robins return
Shorter days
Firewood
Stew
Walnuts
Sleeping in

•

Recipes

The heat, for what it is, breaks. The mornings are cooler. Porridge simmers. Sometimes the first frost hits in early March. With it, the insects (well, some of the insects) drop in number. A natural pesticide, the chill freezes the troughs and numbs my hands when I milk but knocks the cabbage moths for a six.

Often, we get more calm days in autumn. As the wind eases, we busy ourselves. With firewood. With splitters and chainsaws and stacking wood. It's this wood that will fire not only our heater and cooker in the house, but also the cooker (Bessie the Esse), the wood oven (The Dennis) and our fire pit at the restaurant. We thrive on ancient cooking techniques, where it's the cook and raw materials that decide the flavour, not a sous-vide machine and a digital thermometer.

Autumn is always a time to take stock, to draw breath after the madness of summer. By now, the glut of cucumbers is pickled, the surfeit of berries jammed, the busy tourist season easing. Yes, we still have passata to make as the tomatoes continue to give, yet mostly it's the pomme fruit – the apples, pears and quince – that occupy our kitchen time. With over thirty varieties of apples alone, the harvest, and the use, requires attention. They're forgiving fruit, and much is turned into cider, and, later still, some to vinegar. The vinegar is used to keep our livestock healthy, to pickle, to cook with. The cider, too, is a regular companion in the kitchen, and not always in the pot.

Our valley, and other valleys nearby, look exquisite as autumn strikes and the deciduous trees dress in colour. Like them, we take a moment to rejuvenate, to draw in deeply. The soil cools as the light drops. Growth in the garden slows, almost grinding to a halt. Grass and weeds follow suit. We await the winter rains, knowing they will come, though never quite sure of the exact date and if it'll start in autumn. As we wait, we ready fences, secure paddocks, move feed, ready for the oncoming mud. This time, a bridge between sunny, fecund summer and foggy, damp winter is always one of bold sunrises that are easily seen even by later risers (by farming standards), especially before the clock reverts to winter hours. This is a time of soups, stews and sticky buns. Of dinner invitations and red wine.

After the summer, autumn is a time to re-establish friendships. To find time for mates. We head to the wild places, to reset our sense of place. And every year, we use this time, of all times, to really understand priorities. Each year we're more thankful of the place we call home.

We feel blessed to live in such a community, where what matters most isn't your job, or your suburb, or your status. What matters is the strength of your familial bonds, your relationship with the world around you, and your generosity at the table. What matters is older and newer than a single day, a single person or a single belief. What matters is the cycle of life, in and on the earth. What matters is humanity itself.

The Autumn

Windfalls. The apples that drop to the ground before we have a chance to pick them. And we really cop a windfall in autumn. The fallen fruit is fed to the pigs; it sweetens the meat, fattens the porkers, ready to turn into prosciutto and pancetta and sausages on our annual pig day. Apples that don't fall are transformed into pies, tarts, apple sauce, cider, syrup. Autumn means the last of the berries, tomatoes, eggplant, zucchini and beans. Late autumn we spy the first broccoli, cauliflower and frost-sweetened kale. Yet, the season is probably best signified by chestnuts, and they look the part with their muted brown colours. Our trees are still in their infancy, their small crop of hoary fruit a reminder of places far afield, and a reminder of crops for the next generation.

Harvest

March.
Kohlrabi, flint corn, the last tomatoes, pumpkins (winter squash), delicata squash. Apples, including Cox's Orange Pippin and its relatives: Ribston Pippin and James Grieve. Pears.

April.
Beetroot (beets), chard (silverbeet), spring onions (scallions), English spinach. Autumn is great for spicy greens: rocket (arugula), dill, coriander (cilantro), mustard greens. Apples, including Bramley's Seedling and Cats Head for cooking. Democrat apples. Rhubarb gives and gives. Chestnuts, quince.

May.
Parsnip, bulbing onions, the first brussels sprouts. The first caulis peer out from under their huge leaves: snowy white or deep purple. Sturmer apples, olives.

16 MARCH

Well, that was dry. The talk around the traps over summer was of feeding out hay, and empty dams, and records broken. We're lucky. In so many other parts of Australia the dry lasts years, the farms run up debt and the mood, not just in the farmhouse but in the community, turns sullen. In our climes, it is temporary. The rains will come as they always do.

A pig has died. More than one. But one in particular stands out. Dorian, The Explorian, the pig that wandered off from mum hours after birth and never attached again, was found dead near the house after nearly three months of hand rearing. No visible signs of injury. Perhaps it was a snake bite.

Other pigs have died too. One was stillborn to Jackie – an underweight, forlorn-looking runt found at the entrance to her shelter. Another crushed the next morning. I find death confronting, demanding, humiliating. In these moments, I almost understand the farrowing crate, the cage that birthing mothers (farrowing sows, in industry speak) are kept housed in, at intensive farms, for three to four weeks of their life. I understand the heartbreak for the owner, or the workers, to have to find a series of dead piglets each morning. A hundred new mothers, maybe a hundred dead slips. All in a morning's work.

I know that even wild pigs, with a litter of only four or five, may also crush their young. I know that over the years our crush rate is the same as shedded pigs whose mothers are effectively incarcerated in farrowing crates. And I know the old adage: if you have livestock, you have dead stock. But still, it breaks my heart. I think if you are immune to this, if you are emotionally neutral at the death of an animal, be it through natural or man-induced causes, then you shouldn't be charged with the care of animals. If you are unmoved by the sight of a dead animal, there is something dead in you.

And yet, as farmers, death surrounds us. It lingers always on the horizon. It haunts our nights when we know birth is due. Grim, joyful, scary, the birth of a mammal is all things at once: a heart stopping, gleeful, anxious time, no different from the birth and replacement of ourselves. Sometimes we get to play God. Sometimes God gets to play God. Today, if there is a God, then he or she definitely had a hand in the death of Dorian. And curse his hand I do.

26
MARCH

The local smallholder's festival was a bit damp after a spot of rain. We took the red van, loaded with spuds and pickled beans and bacon and baked beans that had sat, melting to buttery softness, in the oven overnight. Next to us, Deep End Farm had their amazing pork bao, along with a beef version of the steamed Taiwanese bun. Everybody asks about their food, but only few seem interested in the fact the pork is from their own land, free-ranged, tended with love, tended from the moment of birth to the sealing of each dumpling. Vegetarians may not understand this dichotomy, but caring about what we eat is hardwired into us now. We can care for our environment and cut a tree down to build a shed. We can care about our livestock and still eat meat. The two ideas aren't contradictory, or mutually exclusive.

My pockets are laden with sunflower seeds. A snack from the garden that's (nearly) worth the labour of cracking open each seed. The chooks – eventually – will get the bigger share.

9
APRIL

The last of the apples cling tenaciously to the trees, some yet to ripen, most now gone.

I fashion a salty pear tarte tatin to serve alongside ice cream stained with gilded flecks thanks to our neighbour's saffron. We grow most of what we consume, but saffron and pinot noir will never be among our crops. Both take too much land, too much time, and both come from very close, very talented neighbours who specialise in such things.

Nature revels in mid autumn. A white goshawk, strangely pale for a bird in these climes, has been worrying the chooks. Most of the wild birds are brown or brightly robed. Some, like the ducks, are both. Some are dark as pitch, like the occasional yellow-tailed black cockatoo and the ever present, always watching ravens. I admire their attitude: patient, watchful, purposeful. They cascade through the air, doing high dives and sharp turns. They take risks, chasing the wedge-tailed eagles from potential prey, prey that perhaps includes their young. I like the fact that smaller birds can outwit the eagle, or at least out-bore them.

We spy the first ever magpie in a decade of living down south. The first fig, ripened on the tree (which has had five years and plenty of fruit in the last couple of years, but never one so soft as to be worth plucking from the stem). We wonder if these are the visible effects of a changing climate, or are simply new to us. We know from the rain we record that it is getting drier, generally, each year. We also know the ocean currents that circle our island home are rising in temperature three to four times the global average. About 2°C over the last couple of decades. Maybe the maggies are here to stay.

A warm but moist autumn means wild mushrooms. Horse mushrooms, shaggy parasols. So far this year my secret spot for slippery jacks and the occasional saffron milk cap is bearing only fly agarics, the red-and-white spotted 'toadstool' that I suspect would kill us. Or at least render our kidneys useless. Then I spy a single, lonely shaggy ink cap, the short-lived, sweet, elegant-flavoured mushroom that you mustn't eat with alcohol. Apparently it contains the same chemical used to make alcoholics violently ill if they drink while on the medication. I have no desire to test the theory, roasting them in the oven with butter and garlic, and keeping the pinot noir for another day. Another week. Another mushroom.

It's rained again. It rarely rains when we really need it, only after the height of summer is but a mere memory. But this rain is still wanted. The grass is greening underneath, if a bit stagnant after the heat. While the first of the deciduous trees change colour – mostly the early apples and the willows – life still booms in the rest of the farm. The pasture, our soil, needs this rain.

Much of the growth in the paddocks is, however, blackberry. Those thorny, tenacious, deep-rooted weeds that are gradually starting to make inroads into the pasture. Blackberries mean we rely on the goats, because goats are really, really good at eating blackberry plants. And goats have meant better fences, better infrastructure, and a whole new species to get our heads around.

15 APRIL

It's chucked it down. I feel like a fraud. We talk a lot about trying to grow topsoil, about the effect of millennia washing the fertility from our neighbours' land onto our place, and in the space of three days, with about 45 mm of rain, I see a pig paddock turn from a worn but still acceptable home into a potential soil catastrophe.

This is farming on the front line. Visitors see the pretty view. Our neighbours' vines. The South West wilderness, the Huon River, our verdant paddocks (after the golden colour of summer). I see the grass's length, the soil's structure, the water's path. There's no right way to do things long term. Every season is different, and it's how we, as farmers, manage things, how we respond, that will determine how much topsoil we grow, or lose. It's the long game of personal commitment, ethics, world-view, resources and energy levels.

Right now, I'm tired. Burned out. If it wasn't for our staff, I'd lock the gate and bunker down. Thirty months after opening as a restaurant, there have been too many days over 10 hours at chef-like pace (farmers work long hours, but move a little slower – they need the longevity). I head out to do some chores and feel like keeping on driving. Taking to the road, like I did as a young man without land. Without a family. Without responsibility for the families of the people we employ. My job on this farm entails looking at soil health, plant growth, animal welfare, food security, social responsibility, flavour and pleasure. From the microscopic to the esoteric. From the invisible to the global. There's little opportunity for irresponsible use of alcohol in my personal life. No heavy chardonnay drinking and carousing.

This isn't the life I once had. Maybe I grew up too late in life. Maybe I've taken on more than I should. Maybe I'm a lightweight who can't hack it on the land. Doubts. I'm plagued by doubts.

It sometimes feels like a folly, like we don't make progress. That things don't work as they should. Then, the shiitake logs sprout, three years after I inoculated them with spores. And I think how wondrous nature is, and our hand in it. And I eat those shiitakes with elation and look forward to the next challenge on the farm.

7 MAY

Three wedge-tailed eagles are wheeling overhead, the parents teaching the young 'un to hunt. I wonder whether one of our pigs was part of the chick's diet a few months ago, and if it was, so be it. Of course, I'd rather they found native wildlife, of which there's no shortage, and of which I can make no use in our kitchen (thanks to regulations). But I grudge them not. No, if a threatened species needs to take the occasional piglet, it's a small price to pay.

The most death I wrought this week was on the brussels sprouts. Thousands of aphids lurk under the leaves of the plant. We peel each sprout, then soak the lot in water to drown out the insects. It's carnage on a scale no one cares about, but it does make me think. If there are no aphids on your sprouts, it probably means somebody, somewhere, has already killed them.

The 100+ km an hour gusts of wind have bent the chimney and loosened the hot water system on the roof. They've pulled down trees, bent metal posts holding wind break cloth, sucked the insulation from underneath the restaurant and ripped off tree guards. They've beaten down the cheery heads of the sunflowers, and lifted the weed mat. They're sending us a bit barmy with their unrelenting noise, but, strangely, inside it feels too still. Unnervingly still. An eerie calm after being immersed in nature's power.

We borrow a laser level and mark out swales. These long drains closely follow the contour, trapping water as it comes down the hills, slowing it down to decrease erosion, and trapping it in places it may otherwise not be, meaning we can grow more, with the same rainfall, on the same land. I marvel at the power of diesel. We build three swales in a day using a digger and Mal's driving skills. As we finish, the skies open, and in the space of a few hours I can see we've managed to angle the swales correctly. A relief it is.

Elsie still enjoys a rub, months after her retirement from the dairy.

9

MAY

Evita, one of our sows, has given birth. Eight healthy piglets born, thankfully, in her little shelter. They stay hidden beneath the hay. I hope the eagles don't spy them there.

11

MAY

I lie in bed and listen to the rain on the roof. In summer, when rain is scarce and the paddocks desiccate, the sound is reassuring. I imagine the dampness seeping into the soil, moistening and nourishing plants and grass alike. A good deluge can help recharge the dams and invigorate the paddocks while rejuvenating our souls. Today, though, I wake to the sound of a gale blowing overhead. I feel the house shudder with the force of the wind, and the rain is tumbling, cascading down in torrents. We hope it's not as bad as the worst autumn and winter, when it didn't seem to stop raining for months, and the sound of the drops drumming on the tin roof started to sink my heart and test my soul – knowing that the rain would cause mud of heroic proportions, that the pigs would go from happy to sodden, and that the ground we are custodians of would get damaged by every trotter, hoof or snout; even our boot-clad feet would injure the soil.

But that was a decade ago, and this downpour in late autumn scares me with the wind's ferocity and scale, but we wake to find the farm in good nick. Yes, a pig shelter is tipped on its side, there are rivulets in places that don't normally have them, like the middle of the driveway, but all up, we dodged the worst of it as the winds gnarled in from the east. The brassicas – cabbage, cauli, broccoli and kale – have survived the blow. So too the broad beans, though they're only in their infancy. A drive to our town of Cygnet, just over the brow of the hill, shows a different story. Trees with their tops ripped out. Whole gums lying at the road's edge, sawn off already by a thinking neighbour who left their farm at dawn with a chainsaw at hand, knowing what might await. We see loose tin on sheds, gardens blown away, orchards harmed. Yes, this time, we got off lucky.

27
MAY

It's late this year. The first frost, which crisps on the windscreen while I light the oven before dawn. One year, the first frost was in February. Usually, it's early March.

The cold sometimes bites, sometimes creeps, the feeling seeping from my fingers as I move cows and feed pigs, so by the time I'm done my hands feel like clubs on the ends of my arms.

The rain has belted down, washing whole garden beds away at farms not too far away. Two hundred and forty millimetres at some, 50 mm a couple of kilometres away. Eighty-seven millimetres here. The chimney is now seriously skewwhiff. We missed the worst of it again, but this time we're not unscathed.

The goats, supposedly an animal that seeks shelter (though theirs remains steadfastly unused), are seemingly oblivious to it all.

Aloof, nervous, yet inquisitive and alert, they change the landscape merely by their looks. I watch over them as they do exactly as we'd hoped, nibbling the blackberries that are encroaching, little by little, on the paddocks.

Our new dairy matriarch, Myrtle, gives me litres of milk, though the calf has learned to suckle as I approach, always trying to anticipate my timing for the overnight separation. Go on then, one last drink of warm milk before bed.

We harvested the last tomatoes in mid May. The last fig on the 20th of May. Yet the brussels sprouts, a classic winter crop, which took up home in the garden in late December, have also been on the menu for weeks. Nature is unreliable. The frost, that deep, biting cold that stings the cheeks when you ride on the back of the ute, that icy morning snap, will help kill the aphids that still feast on the outside of the brussels. Frost, but only when it stops raining and blowing.

I stand and look at flowers that we grow in the garden and pretty soon count more than fifty hoverflies, natives to Tasmania, that not only pollinate crops, but also can predate on the aphids. I start to understand the ecology of our farm a little more. As Dr Simon Grove, head of invertebrates at the local museum says, all farming, even our style of organic farming, is an alien environment on this land. But insects, those millions of species, most of which are yet to be identified by science, are integral to a healthy ecosystem, including the one we're building on this patch of land. We plant flowers to encourage insects. We build insect hotels. We build communities of microbes, plants, invertebrates, birds and marsupials on Fat Pig Farm. In our aim to help strengthen our small community of like-minded souls, we've found we've built communities of creatures, of people, and there is resonance sometimes from way beyond the fence line of our farm, the coastline of our state, the island we call home.

Real Shepherd's Pie

Serves 6

Shepherds ate lamb and potato pie before there was such a thing as 'shepherd's pie'. This is my version, using leftover roast lamb; if you use beef, it's cottage pie.

40 g (1½ oz) butter

3 onions, peeled and finely diced

3 carrots, peeled and finely diced

4 celery stalks, finely diced

500 g (1 lb 2 oz) leftover cooked lamb, finely diced

125 ml (4 fl oz/½ cup) Worcestershire sauce

2 tablespoons tomato sauce (ketchup) or paste (concentrated purée)

1 tablespoon white-wine vinegar

1 thyme sprig

1 bay leaf

1 kg (2 lb 3 oz) mashed potato, whatever way you like it

Heat the butter in a large saucepan and fry the vegetables for about 10 minutes until soft, without allowing them to darken much.

Add the lamb, stir in all the remaining ingredients except the potato, plus 250 ml (8½ fl oz/1 cup) water and simmer for about 1 hour until everything is soft and cohesive. The mixture should be wet, but not runny.

Preheat the oven to 200°C (400°F).

Spread evenly over the base of a large casserole dish, spoon the mash on top and run a fork over the surface to create a ridged pattern. Brush with butter if you like. Bake for 20–30 minutes, or until lightly coloured.

L'Aligot

Serves 6

L'Aligot is a French dish of stretchy, smooth potato whipped with a fresh cheese. It's a bit physical to make by hand, but it's kind of fun to do – it's a little like adult playdough.

1 kg (2 lb 3 oz) starchy potatoes, peeled

2–3 garlic cloves, peeled

250 ml (8½ fl oz/1 cup) full-cream (whole) milk

150 g (5½ oz) butter

300 g (10½ oz) provolone or other mild melting cheese, grated

Steam the potatoes with the garlic cloves. When the potatoes are cooked, mash them with the garlic as finely as possible.

Put the milk in a large, heavy-based saucepan. Bring to the boil. Vigorously beat in the potato, a spoonful at a time, with the butter. Turn down the heat. Beat until the potato is light and fluffy. You can use a hand-held mixer if it's strong enough, or plop it into a food processor.

Sprinkle in the cheese, beating the whole time. The mixture will take on a gloss and come away from the side of the pan as you beat it. It is then that it should be eaten, or left ready to reheat later.

Serve with just-steamed veg or, if you've the constitution, with oven-crisped confit, pan-fried Toulouse sausage or some braised smoked ham hock. Leftovers are best pan-fried.

Dill Carrots

Serves 6

Simple, effective and totally delicious, this approach relies on amazingly good, sweet carrots. The dish is pretty nice with tarragon too, in place of the dill, but tarragon can overwhelm more easily, so cut the amount you use to about half.

1 kg (2 lb 3 oz) baby carrots, scrubbed

50 g (1¾ oz) cultured butter

1–2 teaspoons salt, to taste

3–4 tablespoons chopped fresh dill

Steam the carrots until tender.

While the carrots cook, heat the butter in a large saucepan over a low heat. Add the salt, some freshly ground black pepper and, just before the carrots are ready, turn up the heat. Toss in the steamed carrots, stir through the dill and check for seasoning.

Serve hot as a side dish.

Pot-roasted Leeks with Lemon

Serves 6

Really nice, especially with goat's cheese or leftover ham for meat eaters. Use crusty bread and the following sauce for full effect.

6 medium leeks, pale parts only, cleaned well

1 lemon, cut into slices

2 bay leaves

1 thyme sprig (dried is okay, fresh is better)

250 ml (8½ fl oz/1 cup) extra-virgin olive oil

Mayonnaise

2 free-range egg yolks

2 teaspoons dijon mustard

oil drained from the leeks

2 tablespoons tiny capers, rinsed

2 tablespoons gherkins (pickles), chopped

extra lemon juice, if needed

Preheat the oven to 150°C (300°F).

Halve the leeks lengthways and lay in a shallow casserole dish. Dot with lemon slices, add the remaining ingredients and some salt and pepper. Cover with baking paper, then foil, and bake for about 30–40 minutes, or until the leeks are tender. (The cooking time can vary a lot depending on how old the leeks are.) Drain the oil (see Tip) and any cooking juices, discard the thyme, bay leaves and lemon slices and serve.

Tip

Here's a nice sauce made using the leftover lemony leek olive oil.

Make a mayonnaise by whisking the egg yolks and mustard together, then very gradually whisking in the oil. Add the capers and gherkins and season to taste, adding more lemon juice if needed.

Warm Potatoes with Dill Mustard Butter

Serves 6

You could just use the butter with a piece of veal or fish, but I like the excellent way it moistens potatoes.

1 kg (2 lb 3 oz) pink eye, kipfler (fingerling) or other waxy potatoes

100 (3½ oz)–150 g (5½ oz) cultured butter, softened

3–4 tablespoons dijon mustard

2 teaspoons lemon juice

2–3 tablespoons chopped fresh dill

Scrub the potatoes well and cut if they're too big (I like to leave them whole if they're small enough). Pop into a big saucepan with cold, salted water, cover and bring to the boil. Reduce the heat and simmer until tender.

While the spuds cook, mash the butter with the mustard and lemon juice until combined. Mash in the dill. Toss the spuds with the butter and add enough salt and pepper to make it taste fab. Serve with a nice piece of grilled fish, some roasted pork, or even a little minute steak.

Rag Pasta with Sausage

Serves 4

A pure pork sausage, scented with fennel, is a lovely thing. It's different from fresh mince with fennel seed added, though you could, at a pinch, substitute that instead. Lean mince or sausages will give an unsatisfactory result, but you can adjust it a little by adding more olive oil at the end.

1 tablespoon olive oil

2 garlic cloves, crushed

400 g (14 oz) tinned peeled tomatoes, or passata

40 g (1½ oz) salt

200 g (7 oz) minced (ground) pork and fennel sausage mince (or use 200 g/7 oz pork sausage meat and 1 tablespoon crushed fennel seeds)

500 g (1 lb 2 oz) Home-made Pasta (page 304), cut into rough shapes

good grating of ewe's milk cheese (such as mild pecorino), or grana padano, to serve

Make the sauce by heating the olive oil in a small frying pan and frying the garlic gently for a minute.

Add the tomatoes (crush them with the back of a spoon) and simmer for 10 minutes. It helps to work a bit quickly at this point.

Put 4 litres (135 fl oz/16 cups) water in a stockpot with the salt and bring to the boil.

With the tomato sauce simmering, crumble in the sausage meat and cook through. As it simmers, cook the pasta in the rapidly boiling water, just until it's close to cooked, then drain, reserving some of the cooking liquid in case the pasta gets a bit dry.

Stir the nearly cooked pasta into the sauce. Continuously stir the pasta over a medium heat to coat with the sauce and allow it to finish cooking. Serve with the grated cheese and freshly ground black pepper.

Pork and Tomatillo Stew

Serves 4 with rice

We grow these amazing green tomatillos and, until recently, only had enough for a bit of salsa. This stew uses just about everything from the farm and tastes heavenly. You can make the Roasted Tomatillo Salsa (page 195) and simply use that with grated zucchini to cook the pork for the last 20 minutes or so.

- a small amount of pork fat
- 600 g (1 lb 5 oz) skinless pork belly or shoulder, diced
- 2 onions, diced
- 2 garlic cloves, crushed
- ½ teaspoon ground cumin
- 1 tablespoon dried oregano
- ¼ teaspoon chipotle powder
- 1 teaspoon salt
- 500 g (1 lb 2 oz) waxy potatoes, diced
- 500 g (1 lb 2 oz) tomatillos, roasted
- 2 zucchini (courgettes), grated
- fresh coriander (cilantro), chopped
- cooked rice, to serve

Heat the pork fat in a large, heavy-based saucepan over a high heat and fry the pork belly well on all sides until brown and the fat has rendered. Drain off some of the fat if it's excessive, remove the pork from the pan and keep to one side.

In the same pan, fry the onion over a medium-low heat until brown. Add the garlic and cook for another minute. Add the cumin and fry for just a few seconds, then add the oregano, chipotle powder, 500 ml (17 fl oz/2 cups) water, the salt and the pork. Bring to the boil, cover with a lid, then reduce the heat to a very low simmer and cook for about 1½ hours, or until nearly tender.

Add the potatoes, tomatillos and zucchini, and cook for another 20 minutes or so until the potatoes are cooked through. Taste for seasoning and toss in a good handful of coriander.

Serve warm with rice.

A Right and Proper Apple Pie

Serves 6–8

My gran used to be so worried about the apple going tough in her rightly famed apple pie that she'd prise the lid off the pie halfway through cooking to add the sugar. I don't usually go to the bother, but I admire her for doing just that.

750 g (1 lb 11 oz) Lard Shortcrust Pastry (page 301)

100 g (3½ oz) caster (superfine) sugar

750 g (1 lb 11 oz) cooking apples (golden delicious or granny smith are good common varieties), peeled, cored and sliced thinly

1 teaspoon finely grated lemon zest

6 whole cloves

1 small free-range egg, lightly beaten with a pinch of salt

cream, custard or ice cream, to serve

Rest the pastry for 1 hour after making it.

Preheat the oven to 200°C (400°F).

Roll out two-thirds of the pastry and line the base of a greased 25 cm (10 in), 5 cm (2 in) deep pie dish. Sprinkle the pastry with 2 teaspoons of the sugar. Toss the apple with the remaining sugar, lemon zest and cloves, then press into place in the pastry case. Roll out the remaining pastry to fit the top of the pie and press the edges to seal. Cut a slit in the top to allow steam to escape.

Brush the top of the pie with the beaten egg.

Bake in the centre of the oven for 35–45 minutes until the pastry is cooked. Serve warm with cream, custard or ice cream.

Pear, Walnut and Treacle Tart

Serves 6–8

Yes, it is a bit of mucking around shelling your own walnuts, but this tart tastes twice as good if you can be bothered to put in the effort.

200 g (7 oz) Sweet Shortcrust Pastry (approx. half of the recipe on page 302)

200 g (7 oz) walnut pieces (from about 500 g/1 lb 2 oz whole nuts)

40 g (1½ oz) (about 2 slices) white bread, soaked in a little milk to soften, then squeezed dry and mushed up

100 g (3½ oz) treacle

1 teaspoon finely grated mandarin zest (freeze the fruit for a little while to get the skin to firm up if needed)

2 free-range egg yolks

100 g (3½ oz) poached pears, cored and cut into eighths

thick (double/heavy) cream, to serve

Preheat the oven to 180°C (350°F).

Line an 18 cm (7 in) flan tin (one that will allow you to get the tart out easily when cooked) with the pastry and blind-bake (see Note on page 109). Once done, keep the oven at 180°C (350°F).

Scatter 50 g (1¾ oz) of the nuts evenly over the pastry.

In a food processor, grind the remaining nuts to a fine crumb, pulse in the bread and place in a bowl. Add the treacle, zest and yolks, and mix well.

Pour into the pastry case, press in the pear segments gently, ensuring they're evenly spaced, and bake for 20–25 minutes, or until set. Allow to cool before removing from the tin. Serve at room temperature with double cream.

Potato Gnocchi with Ragu

Serves 4

Perfect gnocchi are light, not rubbery. They taste of potato. They're like edible clouds. Less than perfect gnocchi are doughy. Gluey. Starchy. A lot comes down to how you cook and mash the potato, and how much you work the dough. And practice, as in all things, makes perfect. After a few goes, you can ditch the egg, a binder that is a really good safety net for beginners, but is scoffed at in some parts of Italy.

1 kg (2 lb 3 oz) large desiree or other slightly starchy potatoes

200 g (7 oz/1⅓ cups) plain (all-purpose) flour, plus extra for dusting

1 free-range egg (optional)

1 tablespoon salt

olive oil, for tossing

100 g (3½ oz) An Italian Meat Ragu (page 280)

50 g (1¾ oz) butter

50 g (1¾ oz/½ cup) grated parmesan

Preheat the oven to 200°C (400°F).

Scrub the potatoes and bake until soft, about an hour. Then you're going to have to work quickly. Hot potatoes are, well, like handling hot potatoes, and they need to be hot to make the best gnocchi.

Quickly peel the spuds. You can use a tea towel (dish towel) if they are too hot to handle. (Alternatively, I like to cut them in half and scoop out the flesh with a spoon.) Put this through a potato ricer while still hot (alternatively, pass through a fine-mesh sieve, but that's wearisome and slow), and quickly fold in the flour. Just mix it enough so that it comes together. If adding the egg, add it after the flour is partially mixed in.

Work just until it's smooth. No longer, or it'll go gluey. Cut into six pieces and roll each sixth on a lightly floured bench under your hands to make a long, even sausage shape about 1.3 cm (½ in) in diameter. Cut each of these logs into little pieces, about 1.2 cm (½ in) long. These are your gnocchi. You can round them with your hands and press a fork into each one to create ridges on one side to absorb more sauce, but that's up to you.

Heat 2 litres (68 fl oz/8 cups) water in a large, wide stockpot over a very high heat and add the salt. Bring to the boil, then add half the gnocchi, stirring as you go to ensure they don't stick together. When they float, give them another 10–20 seconds then scoop them out with a slotted spoon, draining well, and tossing into a bowl with just a tiny bit of oil. Repeat with the remaining gnocchi.

Heat the ragu with the butter, toss in the gnocchi, and spoon it around to coat well. Serve in four dishes, with the parmesan on top.

Roast Garlic and Onion Soup

Serves 4

In this variation on the Provencale garlic soup, you char the onions and garlic to give them a roasted, toasty flavour, then purée to make a soup. It really does taste of garlic, so use the best-quality local garlic you can afford and you won't see a vampire all week. You can whisk the egg with some grated gruyère to enrich the dish even more.

2 red onions, unpeeled

10 garlic cloves, unpeeled

3 fresh thyme sprigs

2–3 fresh bay leaves

about 20 fresh sage leaves

¾ teaspoon salt

4 slices bread

4 fresh, free-range eggs

80 ml (2½ fl oz/⅓ cup) extra-virgin olive oil

Place the whole, unpeeled onions in the embers of a fire and cook, turning a few times, until the insides are tender and the outsides blackened. The trick is to scorch the outer leaves so the smoky flavour infuses the centre. To do this in a conventional kitchen, place the onions directly on a gas flame, or even an electric element, to scorch the outside, then bake in an oven preheated to 200°C (400°F) for about 30 minutes, or until soft.

Roast the garlic in a dry frying pan over a moderate heat, tossing regularly to scorch the outside while the middle cooks.

Peel the scorched outside off the onions and garlic and purée well to a paste. Place the paste in a saucepan, add about 1 litre (34 fl oz/4 cups) water and simmer with the thyme, bay leaves and half the sage for 15 minutes. Add the salt and some black pepper, then taste for seasoning.

Char the bread over a flame or in a hot chargrill pan. It's important that it's dark for flavour, not just a bit of limp toast. You can dry-fry it in a heavy-based frying pan too, and get that subtle but essential charry flavour.

Place the hot bread in the base of four bowls and crack the eggs over. Working quickly, scatter the remaining sage leaves over the top. Add the olive oil to the still-boiling soup, then remove from the heat and quickly spoon the soup over the bread and egg. The boiling soup cooks the egg a bit and thickens and enriches the broth. Serve immediately.

Bacon Baked Beans

Serves 6

Oftentimes, we serve a dark, rich baked bean dish, which is nothing like the kind you get in a tin. And often, we're asked for the recipe. This, then, is it.

300 g (10½ oz) dried white beans (northern beans or haricots are fine)

2 fresh bay leaves

1 teaspoon salt

400 g (14 oz) smoky bacon cut into large, fat chunks – fatty bacon is perfect for this

400 g (14 oz) tinned chopped tomatoes

2 large onions, peeled and diced

5–6 garlic cloves, peeled

2 tablespoons treacle, plus more for finishing

Soak the white beans overnight if possible. Drain and place them in a large saucepan with the bay leaves and salt. Cover with enough water so that the beans are about 2 cm (¾ in) beneath the surface. Set over a shockingly large flame and bring to the boil, then reduce the heat and barely simmer for about 60 minutes to 1½ hours, or until the beans are nearly, but not quite fully, cooked. Stir the beans as they cook, and add more water so they are always fully submerged. Drain and keep both the beans and the cooking water.

Preheat the oven to 200°C (400°F).

In a large casserole, combine the beans (with the bay leaves), the bacon, tomato, onion, garlic, some freshly ground pepper and the treacle. Add enough of the bean cooking water to ensure the beans are just covered but not swimming around. Cover the pot with a tight-fitting lid (you could use baking paper and foil in the absence of a lid).

Place in the oven and cook for 30 minutes, then reduce the temperature to about 110°C (230°F). Cook for another 3–4 hours, or until the beans are swollen and buttery soft. Taste for salt. (Remember, the bacon added salt and there was already salt in the bean cooking water.) The beans should be smoky, rich and a little bittersweet. You can adjust with more treacle if needed.

Allow to sit for a few minutes, adding a touch more water if they are too dry, and serve hot. They keep really well for a week in the fridge, too, but often need a splash more water when you go to reheat them.

The Pecking Order

Sebastian looks the part. He has long tail feathers, a proud comb, and struts the orchard like he owns the joint. In a way, he does.

Sebastian is our rooster. A cracking-looking light Sussex, he's got a full-throated crow, seven girls to watch out for, and a dominion of a hundred square metres to patrol. You don't need a rooster to get eggs for the frying pan, but a farm without a rooster feels like a farm without soul.

Keeping chickens was the reason I moved to Tassie. It's the reason I started to wonder about the origins of our food. When I had chooks as a kid, in a fenced-in, barren corner of our yard, the eggs, despite the birds' lack of fresh pasture and attendant grubs to eat, were amazing. I missed those eggs, and never, not even at the most expensive restaurants in the country, came close to getting an egg as good as in my childhood. So I moved to somewhere I could have chooks (though it was also somewhere I could have a cow and sheep and pigs ...).

And the result? Eggs as good as my childhood memories. Eggs with firm whites, rich yolks, and a complex, intense, incomparable flavour.

Having chooks, like having a garden, isn't just the preserve of farmers. Lots of people have rediscovered the backyard chicken, the original household food recycler, to their benefit. Good eggs make for really easy good cooking.

What do you need for chooks? Like all things, they need food, water, air and a home. Chook's houses need to be predator-proof, so made of chicken wire is a good start. Chooks also need protection from the elements, so a sturdy hutch with bars that they can roost on is a must. The roosts, where the birds will spend the night, need to be about 3 cm in width so the chooks can stand properly.

That's the home. Now food and water. The chickens will mess up their water and stand on an open grain container, so commercial waterers and feeders are good investments. Hang them from the roof of the coop, and you'll help keep them away from mice, and keep the dirt from being scratched into them.

Chooks also need a laying box. These are enclosed spaces, so the bird has some privacy. Old washing-machine tumblers work well for size, and a simple bed of straw or hay is enough to make them comfy while they snuggle into the nest and lay.

Importantly, chickens need company. They have a flock mentality, so the ideal minimum is three birds, and they'll naturally work out a pecking order. Give them kitchen scraps, a good bought grain mix, access to greens and insects, and you should get a year or two's worth of eggs even out of the most industrial laying breeds. One of our chooks lasted nearly a decade, long past her time of gifting us eggs, but still giving us joy as she stalked the ground and worried any grubs in the vicinity.

I could watch chickens for hours. The way they scratch the earth and observe the world. The way they interact with each other, their pecking order. Their dust bathing. The rooster watching the sky for an errant hawk. They all have personalities, chooks. They seem to make sense on a farm. With endless uses for their eggs in the kitchen, they certainly make a lot of sense on ours.

Baked Apples with Home-made Marzipan and Bush Honey

Serves 4

The sweet almond flavour of home-made marzipan is a far cry from the almond essence taste most of us grew up with. Here, it enriches wonderful baked apples to become a signature of the cooler months.

- 100 g (3½ oz/⅔ cup) almonds
- 1 free-range egg white
- 2 tablespoons caster (superfine) sugar
- 4 cooking apples (try golden delicious or granny smith)
- 2 tablespoons sultanas
- 1 tablespoon currants
- 1 teaspoon grated lemon zest
- 2 tablespoons bush honey
- 20 g (¾ oz) butter
- runny cream, cider cream or ice cream, to serve

In a food processor, finely blend the almonds. Add the egg white and continue blending until the mixture is smooth, adding the sugar and a pinch of salt as you go. Don't worry if it becomes a bit hard to mix; you can do the last bit by hand. This makes a sticky marzipan. For a drier one, add another 25 g (1 oz) or so of almonds.

Preheat the oven to 180°C (350°F).

Core the apples using a corer if you have one, or a small knife, from both ends, if you don't. You'll wish you had a corer by the end, I reckon. To stop the skin from blowing apart, use a sharp knife to score it from top to bottom.

Mix the sultanas with the currants and lemon zest. Pack about half the marzipan into the centre of the apples, then top with the fruit, and then the remaining marzipan so it is bulging out the top a bit.

Drizzle the honey over the top and crown this stuffing with a knob of butter. Put 125 ml (4 fl oz/½ cup) water in the base of an ovenproof dish, add the apples and bake for 20–30 minutes, or until they're soft right through. They can take more time or less, depending on what variety of apple you have, how fresh they are and just what the real temperature of your oven is.

Serve with runny cream, cider cream or ice cream.

Honey-roasted Quince

Makes 1 kg (2 lb 3 oz)

The best common quince to cook with are Smyrna, which have a luscious perfume and hold together well when cooked. (Pineapple quince are also common, but don't taste as good, and tend to fall apart when cooked.) They're fantastic just like this, with some cream or ice cream. The cooked quince can be used in the Quince Clafoutis (page 276).

- 4 large or 6 medium whole Smyrna quinces
- 150 g (5½ oz) sugar
- 2 large tablespoons honey
- 1 cinnamon stick
- 2 strips lemon rind taken with a potato peeler
- 1–2 whole star anise

Preheat the oven to 160°C (320°F).

Wash and pat dry the quinces. Halve them if they're particularly large, but you can also leave them whole. Place in a baking tray and pour 400 ml (13½ fl oz) water on top, then sprinkle over the sugar and honey, and add the cinnamon stick, lemon rind and star anise.

Cover tightly with aluminum foil and roast in the oven for 3–4 hours, or until the quinces are tender and both the quince and cooking syrup are a deep ruby-pink.

Take the tray out of the oven, remove the cooked fruit and strain the syrup into a jug or jar. Both will keep well in the fridge for at least a couple of weeks.

Apple and Lemon Flummery

Serves 4

A flummery is a light, whipped dessert, here laced with apple and lemon. It's an inconsequence, a fluff, a nothing. Except in flavour.

- 1 large cooking apple, such as granny smith, peeled, cored and stewed to a soft pulp in its own juices
- 150 ml (5 fl oz) dessert wine (optional)
- zest and juice of 2 big lemons
- 3 teaspoons (about 1 sachet) powdered gelatine
- 4 free-range eggs, separated
- 120 g (4½ oz) caster (superfine) sugar (use 100 g/3½ oz if using dessert wine)
- 150 ml (5 fl oz) pouring (single/light) cream, lightly whipped

Rub the apple pulp through a fine-mesh sieve to create a smooth paste, discarding any bits that don't go through the sieve.

Boil the wine (if using), lemon juice and zest, and add the sieved apple pulp and cook for 1 minute. Whisk in the gelatine until dissolved. While that mixture cools, whisk the egg yolks with half the sugar until pale and light.

In a clean bowl, whisk the egg whites with the remaining sugar until soft peaks form. Fold the cooled apple mixture into the egg yolks, then really gently fold in the whipped cream and the egg whites. Spoon into serving glasses and place in the fridge to set. If it separates just slightly, that's fine, it'll still taste light and lovely.

Beef Goulash

Serves 5–6

We often serve a pork goulash that I published in my *Winter on the Farm* book, which uses more sour cream, but this one uses beef. Substitute pork shoulder if you like.

1–2 tablespoons lard (or beef fat or olive oil), for frying

1 kg (2 lb 3 oz) stewing beef, cut into 2 cm (¾ in) dice

1 tablespoon plain (all-purpose) flour

2 onions, peeled and diced

4 garlic cloves, sliced, crushed or just peeled

40 g (1½ oz) Hungarian sweet paprika

80 ml (2½ fl oz/⅓ cup) tomato passata (puréed tomatoes)

500 ml (17 fl oz/2 cups) water or beef stock

1 teaspoon salt

¼ teaspoon freshly ground black pepper

200 g (7 oz) waxy potatoes, scrubbed and diced

200 g (7 oz) turnips, scrubbed and diced

100 g (3½ oz) sauerkraut

50 g (1¾ oz) sour cream

dill cucumbers, to serve

Heat the lard in a large, preferably ovenproof pot over a lively flame. Dust the beef with the flour and fry the meat until it's browned well all over. It's worth doing this in two batches, but be sure to rub the bottom of the pan with a wooden spoon as you go so the flour doesn't scorch too much. Take the meat out of the pan and put to one side.

To the same pot, add a little more fat and fry the onion over a medium heat until it is starting to colour, stirring often to stop it sticking. Throw in the garlic and stir as it fries for another minute, then add the paprika and cook for a further minute, stirring constantly. Pop the meat back in with the tomato and water and season with the salt and pepper. Stir off any leftover stuck-on bits. Put the lid on, bring to the boil over a high heat, give it a good stir, and then turn the heat right down to a bare simmer for 1½ hours.

Stir the goulash occasionally. Add the potatoes and turnips, push them into the sauce, cover with the lid, and allow the dish to keep cooking until the meat, spuds and turnips are tender – about another 30 minutes. Remove from the heat. Add the sauerkraut and stir to combine well. Stir in the sour cream and taste for seasoning. Serve with the dill cucumbers.

Ajiaco (Bogota Chicken, Corn and Potato Stew)

Serves 4–6

This is my version of the Bogota classic. Part of the secret is to have at least a couple of types of potato, or cut one type differently (some chunks, some diced). Ideally it would include pickled potatoes and guasca, a wild herb unique to Colombia, but this version is actually achievable, even if it's not all that authentic.

50 g (1¾ oz) butter, for frying

1.6 kg (3½ lb) free-range chicken, cut into 8 segments

1 large onion, peeled and diced

2 corn cobs, husks and silks removed, cut into 4 rounds each

1 kg (2 lb 3 oz) potatoes (try about one-third washed new potatoes, one-third desiree washed and cut into chunks, and one-third ordinary washed potatoes), peeled and finely diced

bunch of coriander (cilantro), well washed

80 ml (2½ fl oz/⅓ cup) pouring (single/light) cream, optional

Avocado Salsa (see below), to serve

2 tablespoons capers, rinsed, to serve

Avocado Salsa

1 avocado, diced

1 hard-boiled, free-range egg, diced

good handful of coriander (cilantro) leaves, chopped

2 tablespoons finely chopped spring onion (scallion) or red onion

1 teaspoon white-wine vinegar

a few squirts of Tabasco or other chilli sauce

Heat a knob of butter in a big stockpot over a medium flame and brown the chicken pieces, perhaps in two batches. Remove and keep to one side.

In the same pot, fry the onion until soft, then return the chicken to the pot with the corn, potatoes and coriander stems (including roots if attached). Add enough water to just cover the meat, about 1–1.5 litres (34–51 fl oz/4–6 cups), plus some salt and pepper. Put the lid on and simmer for 10 minutes, then remove the breasts.

Simmer the rest for an hour or more (1½ hours is good), then remove the coriander stems and return the breast meat to the pan. Tip in the cream and simmer for another 5 minutes.

To make the salsa, combine all the ingredients in a bowl and season with salt and pepper to taste.

Chop the coriander leaves and toss into the stew pot, then serve with capers and salsa.

Quince Clafoutis

Serves 4

A clafoutis is a batter-based dessert that houses fruit – usually dark cherries or sour cherries – but you can do it with pears or figs, or the like. It works really well with cooked quince, too, which is one of our favoured ways to make use of the autumn fruit.

2 tablespoons melted butter, plus extra for greasing

2 tablespoons raw (demerara) sugar

2 free-range eggs

250 ml (8½ fl oz/1 cup) full-cream (whole) milk

50 g (1¾ oz) caster (superfine) sugar

50 g (1¾ oz/⅓ cup) plain (all-purpose) flour

1 teaspoon grated lemon zest

½ teaspoon vanilla extract

200 g (7 oz) Honey-roasted Quince (page 270), peeled, cored and cut into 1 cm (½ in), or slightly larger, dice

whipped cream or ice cream, to serve

Preheat the oven to 200°C (400°F).

Take a wide, flat, 1 litre (34 fl oz/4 cup) ovenproof dish or pie dish and grease it with butter. Toss in the raw sugar so that it lines the inside of the dish and sticks to the butter.

Beat the eggs, add the milk and sugar, and stir until dissolved. Stir in the flour, melted butter, lemon zest and vanilla, and whisk until smooth.

Pour this batter into the ovenproof dish, dot the quince evenly all over, and bake for about 25–30 minutes, or until the clafoutis is starting to colour and the centre has set (it should no longer be runny, but probably still has some wobble to it).

Serve warm (not hot) with whipped cream or ice cream.

Think Like a Goat (or a Sheep)

Goats and sheep have only ever been a minor part of what we farm. Their propensity to escape from all but the most secure paddocks, along with the boggy nature of our valley floor location, means that they're harder work than the cows. Their feet need trimming, their mineral needs are high, and if you turn your back they've suddenly become your neighbour's sheep, whether you meant them to visit or not.

It took me a while to understand sheep, and I'm still getting to know goats. Thinking of them as prey creatures, where the best they can do is run faster than the goat or sheep next to them in the face of wolf attack, they make more sense. Goats or sheep can't really muscle their way out of a predator's way. They can't kick or charge like a cow or bull. They can't escape to a burrow. They don't have sharp teeth or brute strength like a pig.

When I look at them now, and see their flocking nature, and their nervous demeanour, I understand better what they might be thinking. They're thinking I might eat them, so move forward, go to the middle of the mob, look inconspicuous, run.

And, well, they might be nervous because, you know, I probably will eat them.

An Italian Meat Ragu

Serves 6 with leftovers

There are lots of ways to make an Italian ragu. This is mine. Inspired by Bologna, the sauce is cooked long and slow, a great thing to do on a day when the weather turns. And a little goes a long way. I make a large amount in autumn or early winter and freeze it in small containers, adding more butter to the sauce when I pull it out, ready to flavour gnocchi or pasta (see pages 262 and 304), or put in a lasagne. Feel free to substitute beef mince if veal mince is unavailable.

100 g (3½ oz) butter

2 onions, finely chopped

2 tablespoons flat-leaf (Italian) parsley, chopped

5 celery stalks, washed, finely diced or minced

200 g (7 oz) carrots, finely diced or minced

750 g (1 lb 11 oz) minced (ground) veal (preferably neck)

500 g (1 lb 2 oz) minced (ground) pork (preferably neck)

1 teaspoon salt

500 ml (17 fl oz/2 cups) full-cream (whole) milk

½ teaspoon freshly grated nutmeg

500 ml (17 fl oz/2 cups) white wine (if it's not good enough to drink, then it's definitely not good enough to reduce down and eat)

800 g (1 lb 12 oz) tinned chopped tomatoes (including juice)

cooked pasta, to serve

Heat the butter gently in a really big, heavy-based saucepan and fry the onion and parsley until the onion is translucent.

Add the celery and carrot and continue to fry for a couple of minutes. Increase the heat to high, add the minces, some cracked pepper and the salt, breaking up the meat as it fries. Cook until the liquid has evaporated.

Stir in the milk, reduce the heat and simmer, stirring occasionally, until the milk has evaporated. It'll take a while, and the wider your pot is, the quicker it will happen. Add the nutmeg and wine, stirring occasionally until it has evaporated, then add the tomatoes and 500 ml (17 fl oz/2 cups) water.

Turn the heat right down and barely simmer for 2–3 hours, stirring occasionally and adding 125 ml (4 fl oz/½ cup) water as needed. It will be fairly rich and not watery by the end. Adjust the salt and pepper to taste and serve with pasta cooked in well-salted water.

James Mele's Pig Day Pork Belly

Serves 8–10

A good mate, James Mele, helps host our pig days, when we turn whole pigs into salami, prosciutto, pancetta and more. He cooks this amazingly delicious dish using a little of the fatty part of the pork belly, and it's one of the best things you can eat.

1 kg (2 lb 3 oz) skinless pork belly

3–4 garlic cloves, chopped

½ teaspoon fennel seeds

1–2 teaspoons chopped rosemary

1–2 teaspoons chilli flakes, or to taste

250 ml (8½ fl oz/1 cup) capsicum (bell pepper) paste, available in jars from good delis

crusty bread, to serve

Cut the pork belly into 1 cm (½ in) batons.

Heat a large frying pan over a medium flame, add the pork belly and render it (so the fat comes out) and fry it until it's just brown. You may need to adjust the heat up or down to get to this point; just ensure the meat is frying but not scorching too much.

Pop in the chopped garlic, fennel seeds, rosemary and chilli flakes and stir to fry until they are just cooked, but not browned. This will only take a minute or two, and let your nose be the guide.

Stir in the capsicum paste and cook for another minute or so, then remove from the heat. The capsicum paste and pork fat will make the sauce, and you don't want the sauce too thick. If it gets too thick, add a small amount of water, just a splash or two to start, to thin the sauce.

Serve straight away with crusty bread.

Mandarin-scented Baked Egg Custard

Serves 3–4

A lovely fragrant hint from the mandarin, matched with the bittersweet top, lifts the humble baked egg custard to great heights. For a more indulgent custard, replace the eggs with eight yolks.

250 ml (8½ fl oz/1 cup) full-cream (whole) milk

250 ml (8½ fl oz/1 cup) pouring (single/light) cream

skin of 1 mandarin, peeled and white pith skimmed off

100 g (3½ oz) sugar

4 free-range eggs, lightly beaten

½–1 teaspoon freshly grated nutmeg

3–4 tablespoons caster (superfine) sugar (optional)

Heat the milk and cream in a saucepan with the mandarin peel until just below simmering. Turn off the heat and allow the mix to sit for 15 minutes, then reheat to just below simmering again.

Preheat the oven to 150°C (300°F).

Beat the sugar and eggs together, then quickly beat in the hot milk mixture. Strain into a small casserole dish, sprinkle the nutmeg on top and stir well.

Place the dish in a deep baking tray, pour in enough boiling water to come one-third of the way up the side, or to the level of the custard, and bake for 30–40 minutes, or until set. The best way to tell if the custard has set is to very lightly bump the tray and see if the custard wobbles much. It shouldn't. Cooking times can vary widely because of the heat of the milk, water and the oven, but once it has set, it will start to bubble and overcook, which alters the texture, but it's still quite edible.

Once cooked, you can sprinkle the sugar evenly over the top and scorch it with a blowtorch, if desired. It's good served slightly warm.

Walnut, Chocolate and Whisky Tart

Serves 8–10

This lovely nutty tart uses a quality pastry that is almost like shortbread. I actually press it into the tin if it's too hard to work, rather than try to roll it.

1 quantity Sweet Shortcrust Pastry (page 302)

250 g (9 oz/2½ cups) walnut halves

100 g (3½ oz) brown sugar

100 g (3½ oz/1 cup) almond meal (ground almonds)

3 tablespoons whisky

2 free-range egg whites

1 whole free-range egg

100 g (3½ oz) dark chocolate, melted with 75 g (2¾ oz) butter

whipped cream, to serve

Preheat the oven to 180°C (350°F).

Line a 26 cm (10¼ in) flan tin or similar with the shortcrust pastry and blind-bake (see Note on page 109). You want to use a tin that will allow you to easily remove the tart when cooked, so a flan tin with a removable base is best.

Once blind-baked, keep the oven at 180°C (350°F).

While the pastry cooks, prepare the filling. In a food processor, grind 100 g (3½ oz/1 cup) of the walnuts until fine. Pour into a bowl, then stir in the sugar and almond meal until evenly distributed. Fold through the whisky and eggs, stirring well, then fold through the chocolate and butter.

Pour into the pastry case and dot with the remaining walnuts. Bake for 10–15 minutes, or until just set. Allow to cool before removing from the tin. Serve at room temperature with a drool of lightly whipped cream.

No-machine Saffron Honey Ice Cream

Serves 8–10

Not everybody has an ice-cream machine, and this eats like ice cream but without the need for the equipment.

300 ml (10 fl oz) pouring (single/light) cream

generous pinch of saffron threads

6 free-range eggs, separated

100 g (3½ oz) honey

300 g (10½ oz) sour cream (don't use 'light' cream)

100 ml (3½ fl oz) glucose syrup, sometimes called corn syrup

Heat half the cream with the saffron in a small saucepan over a low flame. Bring almost to the boil, then turn off the heat, pop a lid on, and let the saffron infuse for about an hour. Repeat the heating process once more, and again let it infuse. Cool in the fridge.

Whisk the egg yolks and honey until pale and light. Stir in the saffron cream, the remaining pouring cream and the sour cream, then continue whisking until you have the texture of very lightly whipped cream.

In a clean bowl, whisk the egg whites with the glucose and a pinch of salt until soft peaks form. Gently fold one-quarter of the egg white into the cream mixture until nearly combined, then fold this lightened mixture into the remaining egg whites until you achieve an even consistency. Scoop and scrape into an ice-cream container and freeze for at least 3–4 hours, ideally more like 10 hours, or until frozen.

It keeps well for a few days in the fridge, but it's best consumed in about 1 week. If it's too hard straight from the freezer, defrost for half an hour in the fridge before scooping.

Lemon and Cardamom Rice Porridge

Serves 4–6

Like rice pudding for breakfast, this is a comforting dish that makes a change from porridge but is still warm and filling and fabulous, perfect for a late morning.

1 litre (34 fl oz/4 cups) full-cream (whole) milk

1 vanilla bean, split lengthways (or use 2 teaspoons vanilla extract)

3 cardamom pods, lightly bruised

3 strips lemon peel taken with a potato peeler

100 g (3½ oz) caster (superfine) sugar

125 g (4½ oz) arborio or other risotto rice

200 g (7 oz) stewed rhubarb, or chopped poached pears, or similar, to serve

Heat the milk, vanilla bean, cardamom, lemon peel and sugar in a saucepan over a medium–high heat until it comes to a simmer.

Add the rice, turn the heat right down and stir every few minutes as it simmers for about 20 minutes or so. Keep simmering, stirring occasionally, until the rice is very soft – about another 5–10 minutes, if that. It will thicken up as it cools.

Remove the vanilla bean, lemon peel and cardamom pods, if you can find them, and let it stand for about 30 minutes or thereabouts. Serve warm or at room temperature with warmed stewed rhubarb or poached pears stirred through at the end.

Mandarin Crêpes Suzette

Serves 4

For quite a while now I've been filling crêpes with a mascarpone mix, which enriches the dish and balances the bold citrus in the sauce. Mandarins are super fragrant, but sweet, so the lemon makes a lovely foil.

1 tablespoon mandarin zest

½ cinnamon stick

1 green cardamom pod

50 g (1¾ oz) sugar,
plus 20 g (¾ oz) extra

juice of 5 large mandarins

juice of 1 lemon

1 tablespoon brandy, Grand Marnier or Cointreau

1 free-range egg white

100 g (3½ oz) Home-made Mascarpone (page 312)

8 Crêpes (page 313)

Pop the mandarin zest in a small saucepan with 60 ml (2 fl oz/ ¼ cup) water and the spices. Bring to the boil, turn off the heat and allow the mixture to sit for 10 minutes. Strain and discard the spices.

Sprinkle the sugar over the base of a frying pan and heat, shaking the pan occasionally, until the sugar melts and starts to caramelise. Add the spiced water and simmer until nearly caramelising again. Add three-quarters of the mandarin juice and continue to reduce until it's about half the original volume. Add the remaining juices, slosh in the brandy and remove from the heat. Flambé if you must.

Whip the egg white with the extra sugar until soft peaks form, then fold into the mascarpone. When the sauce is ready, spread the mascarpone mixture thinly on the crêpes, fold into quarters, place on plates and spoon the sauce over.

Salty Pear Tarte Tatin

Serves 8

I have a dedicated 25 cm (10 in) wide cast-iron tatin pan that I carried back from France. More fool me. In Lamotte-Beuvron, where the Tatin sisters created the dish in the Loire Valley, they use a very large, lined springform tin. Simply use a cast-iron or other heavy pan to make the caramel and pears, then transfer it all to the springform tin. (You'll need to make extra caramel to make up for the bit that gets stuck to the frying pan.) I, however, like to think my pan works better. You can make the same dish more traditionally with apples if you like, and Golden Delicious are the best variety.

50 g (1¾ oz) butter

6 firm pears (beurre bosc are best for cooking), peeled, halved and cored

2 fresh bay leaves

1 teaspoon salt

150 g (5½ oz) sugar

1 quantity Pâté Brisee (page 303), rolled to ½ cm (¼ in)

vanilla ice cream, to serve

Heat the butter in a heavy-based 25 cm (10 in) ovenproof frying pan over a low heat. Add the pears, cut side down at first, along with the bay leaves, and cook really slowly to cook and caramelise at the same time. Move them around the pan to make use of any hot and cold spots, and to stop the butter from burning. You may not fit all the halved pears in the pan at the start, but squash them up as they soften and squeeze more in. Sprinkle the salt over evenly as they cook.

When the pears are brown, turn them over and cook the other side, pouring the sugar into the gaps between the pears just as you turn them. Keep cooking over a low heat until the sugar starts to caramelise and the pears are nearly cooked through – a tiny splash of water will slow the sugar caramelising if the pears are still firm. If you've made an apple tarte tatin, you'll find you use less water with pears. Again, you'll need to jiggle the pan and the pears at this stage to avoid hot spots.

Preheat the oven to 200°C (400°F).

When the caramel is dark and thick, and the pears are tender but not soggy, remove the pan from the flame. Cover with the rolled-out pastry, carefully pushing it down around the outside of the fruit, then bake for about 20–30 minutes, or until the pastry is well browned.

When it comes out of the oven, cover with a large plate and invert immediately, ready for serving. Serve warm with vanilla ice cream, or at room temperature later the same day.

Apple Fritters

Serves 4

This wonderful recipe, adapted from Claudia Roden's *The Book of Jewish Food* and introduced to me by the appropriately named and equally wonderful cook Jo Cook, pairs heavenly with vanilla ice cream. The recipe says that it serves four, and it looks like a lot to eat, but somehow four people always manage to get through them all. They remind me of the apple fritters I used to have at the Chinese restaurant at the RSL on Friday nights growing up, though these are much more elegant.

4 sharp-flavoured apples (granny smith or golden delicious work well)

2 tablespoons caster (superfine) sugar, plus extra for sprinkling

3 tablespoons brandy or dark rum

2 free-range eggs, separated

2 tablespoons vegetable oil

150 g (5½ oz/1 cup) plain (all-purpose) flour

200 ml (7 fl oz) cider

vegetable oil, for frying

Core and peel the apples, then cut each into four thick slices through the core so you get rings.

Toss the apple slices in a shallow dish with the sugar and brandy so they're well coated. Leave for 1 hour to macerate, tossing occasionally.

For the batter, beat the egg yolks with the oil and a good pinch of salt. Alternately beat in the flour and cider in small amounts until you have a smooth batter. Leave for 1 hour. Beat the egg whites until stiff, then fold into the batter.

Heat at least 2 cm (¾ oz) of oil in a large frying pan or wok until it reaches about 160°C (320°F) on a cooking thermometer. Dip the apple slices in the batter, working with about five at a time, making sure that they are well covered with batter. Lower each slice carefully into the hot oil. The oil must be sizzling gently, but not too hot or the fritters will brown before the apple is soft inside. It may take a little practice to get it right.

Fry the apple fritters in batches, turning the slices over to brown both sides. Lift out with a slotted spatula and drain on paper towel before serving. Sprinkle with extra sugar or cinnamon sugar (see Note) while warm and serve with a really good-quality vanilla ice cream.

Note

Simply combine 1 tablespoon ground cinnamon with 100 g (3½ oz) caster (superfine) sugar.

Sticky Buns

Makes 8

Heady with a little cardamom, in the style of a Swedish bun rather than a straight cinnamon bun, these are the perfect little mid-morning treats. Or afternoon snacks. Or dinner, if all else in the house has been eaten. The dough is very soft, which makes it a little tricky to work with, but it makes very light buns. An easier dough to work would use only 300 ml (10 fl oz) of milk.

175 g (6 oz) butter, plus extra for greasing

375 ml (12½ fl oz/1½ cups) full-cream (whole) milk

500 g (1 lb 2 oz/3⅓ cups) plain (all-purpose) flour, plus extra for dusting

7 g (¼ oz) sachet active dried yeast

80 g (2¾ oz) caster (superfine) sugar

1½ teaspoons salt

2 teaspoons ground cardamom

1 free-range egg, lightly beaten

100 g (3½ oz) brown sugar

2 teaspoons ground cinnamon

Grease and line a 27 cm (10¾ in) round cake tin.

Combine 65 g (2¼ oz) of the butter with the milk in a small saucepan and heat over a low flame until warm, but not hot to the touch.

In the bowl of a freestanding electric mixer, place the flour, yeast, sugar, ½ teaspoon of the salt and the cardamom. Make a well in the middle of the dry ingredients and add the beaten egg and the warm milk. You don't want hot milk, or it might kill the yeast. Too cold and it will take longer to rise. Use a dough hook to mix it up as much as you can for 5 minutes. It will start to come away from the bowl after a few minutes, but don't worry if it doesn't. All will be good. If you're doing this by hand, just beat as much as you can with a wooden spoon.

Cover this mixture with a tea towel (dish towel) and leave in a warmish place for about an hour, or until it has nearly doubled in size. While this happens, whip the remaining butter, softened, with the brown sugar, cinnamon and remaining salt until soft and light.

Roll the dough out on a lightly floured board to about 25 × 35 cm (10 × 14 in). Spread the brown sugar mix evenly across the top using a spatula, or even two together. Roll up, starting from the short edge, taking care that the filling doesn't squash out. Cut into eight pieces.

It's going to be quite soft, so handle quickly and carefully. Place each piece, cut side up, in the prepared tin, with one piece at the centre and the other seven around the edge, evenly spaced to allow them to expand.

Cover with a tea towel and leave in a warm place to rise again, only for about 30 minutes this time. You just want the dough to be squashy to the touch, not cold and firm. Preheat the oven to 180°C (350°F).

Bake the sticky buns for 20–25 minutes, or until golden brown. You can brush the top with sugar syrup (see Note) as they come out of the oven if you want a glossier look.

Note

To make a sugar syrup, simply boil equal parts water and sugar until the sugar is dissolved. Use while hot.

One day, all the autumn leaves are gone. The air is impossibly fresh. Glorious winter cycles back again.

Basics

Spuds
Potato Bread
Mayonnaise
Bread Sauce
Pastry Doughs
Pizza Dough
Pasta
Flatbread
Fermented Carrots
Naan
Ciabatta
Lavosh
Paneer
Pastry Cream
Mascarpone
Crêpes

The Perfect Roasted Spuds

Serves 6

To make the best roast spuds, use potatoes such as King Edward or Up to Date, or even White Elephant, which are starchy and not sweet. The general rule of thumb is white potatoes, not yellow-fleshed potatoes (see our potato guide on page 60). Then you want to roughen the outside of the cut spuds so that they absorb just a little more fat than a smooth-cut surface would. And then, the fat and temperature of the oven are important. To this end, here's my way to make the perfect roasted spuds.

1 kg (2 lb 3 oz) potatoes, peeled and cut into chunks about 3 cm (1¼ in) at the most. Chunks that have thick and thin bits, the kind a rounded potato will give you, make for the best variation and cooking.

2 teaspoons salt, plus extra to serve

100 g (3½ oz) beef fat

Preheat the oven to 250°C (480°F).

Place the spuds in a saucepan with the salt and fill with cold water until the spuds are well covered. Cover with a lid and bring to the boil over a super-hot flame, then, as they come to the boil, drain well in a colander.

While they're still hot, pop the potatoes back into the saucepan and, with the lid held tightly on, shake the pan vigorously to roughen up the spuds' surface. You want them to look slightly fuzzy at the edges, not smooth. This loosened outside of the potatoes will allow you to get the best crunchy roasted spuds.

Place the beef fat in a large roasting tin in the oven. Allow the fat to become so hot it's almost smoking, then carefully tip the potatoes in. Roast for 5 minutes, then toss the spuds to coat them well with the fat all over. There should be visible fat in the bottom of the pan. If there's not, add more.

Continue to roast the potatoes for about 30 minutes, stirring every 5–10 minutes or so to help them cook evenly. When they're nicely browned on each side, drain for a few seconds on paper towel, season generously with salt and serve immediately.

Potato Bread

Makes 1 loaf

This bread, which I quite like making into a big potato dumpling shape, is lovely with a bit of caramelised onion and rosemary through it. But this is the basic dough, so you can build from here. It's a gorgeous, soft, fine-textured bread that browns quicker than a 100 per cent wheat loaf, so keep an eye on the temperature.

350 g (12½ oz) starchy potatoes

7 g (¼ oz) sachet active dried yeast

2 tablespoons warm water

250 g (9 oz/1⅔ cups) baker's flour

1–2 tablespoons olive oil

1 teaspoon salt

Peel and steam the potatoes until tender. Mash thoroughly, or use a potato ricer to ensure the mash is free of lumps. Keep it warm while you make dough. (I weighed my mash, and it was about 320 g/11½ oz that I added to the dough.)

Mix the yeast with the warm water to help it dissolve. Place the potatoes in a large bowl (make sure they have cooled to about the same temperature as your hand to ensure they're not so hot that they kill the yeast). Add the yeast mixture and stir. Add the flour, olive oil and salt and knead until the dough is a smooth consistency. Cover the bowl with a clean tea towel (dish towel) and allow the mixture to rise for about 2 hours in a nice warm spot. Knead again and shape the dough or place it in a loaf (bar) tin. Allow to rise for 45 minutes or so until it has nearly doubled in size.

Preheat the oven to 220°C (430°F).

Bake the bread for 25 minutes, then turn the oven down to 180°C (350°F) and continue to bake for a further 10 minutes. The bread should be golden and cooked through. Allow to cool for a few minutes in the tin or on a tray, then transfer to a wire rack or similar to cool completely.

Mayonnaise

Makes approx. 250 g (9 oz/1 cup)

I think everybody should know how to make mayonnaise. Here's my basic recipe, which is very versatile and not as hard to knock up as many make out.

2 free-range egg yolks

1 teaspoon French-style or other smooth, mild mustard

1–2 teaspoons lemon juice or white-wine vinegar

250 ml (8½ fl oz/1 cup) oil (200 ml/ 7 fl oz vegetable oil to 50 ml/1¾ fl oz good-quality olive oil)

Pop the egg yolks in a mortar, large bowl or food processor. Mash in the mustard and lemon juice, then season with salt and pepper.

Place the oil in a jug with a spout. Gradually pour the oil into the eggs, whisking or blending constantly, in a thin stream. The idea is to emulsify the oil using the yolks, and if you pour it in too quickly, the oil may separate (see Note). It's easier if you have a friend to hold the bowl, or put a tea towel (dish towel) over a saucepan and place the bowl over that to stop it from spinning. Continue whisking until all the oil has been added. Taste for salt, pepper and acidity.

Because it's a condiment, it should be a little salty and a little sour. To finish, it's good to whisk in 1 tablespoon hot water to help lighten the texture and stabilise the mixture.

Note

If the mayonnaise splits, place another egg yolk in a bowl and gradually whisk in spoons of the split mayonnaise until it is all incorporated. Do this as soon as you see that it has split. Then keep drizzling any unused oil as per the recipe until it is all emulsified.

Bread Sauce

Makes approx. 400 ml (13½ fl oz)

A fantastic accompaniment to plain roast chicken. For an even better result, tip in some of the cooking juices from the roasting pan to enrich it at the end.

500 ml (17 fl oz/2 cups) full-cream (whole) milk

½ onion, peeled

2 cloves

1 bay leaf

generous pinch of grated nutmeg

pinch of ground allspice (optional)

80 g (2¾ oz/1 cup) fresh white breadcrumbs, made by pulsing crustless bread in a food processor

¼ teaspoon salt

Combine the milk, onion, cloves, bay leaf and spices in a saucepan and bring to the boil. Turn the heat right down and simmer for 10 minutes. Remove from the heat and allow to cool for 10 minutes. Reheat and strain into a clean saucepan, discarding the solids. Stir in the breadcrumbs and salt. Bring the mixture back to the boil. Turn off the heat and let it sit for a few minutes so the bread plumps up. It should be pourable, but not thin. Serve hot.

Lemon Bread Sauce

We do vary our bread sauce away from the English style a bit sometimes by adding other things. This lemony, garlicky version goes remarkably well with Jerusalem artichokes (see page 62). To the bread sauce, add the zest of half a lemon and a small clove of crushed garlic as you add the breadcrumbs to the milk.

Lard Yoghurt Pastry

Makes 700 g (1 lb 9 oz)

This is a cracking variation on a yoghurt pastry we've been making for years. Because we have a lot of lard (pork fat) on hand, we love to use it. And because lard gives pastry an incredible flaky texture, we love it even more. Keeping everything chilled – the bowl and flour included – gives the best texture.

- 100 g (3½ oz) lard, chilled and cut into small bits
- 100 g (3½ oz) butter, chilled and diced
- 300 g (10½ oz/2 cups) plain (all-purpose) flour, chilled, plus extra for dusting
- ½ teaspoon salt
- 200 g (7 oz) plain yoghurt, chilled

Using your fingertips (or a food processor), rub the lard and butter into the flour and salt, pulsing if using the processor. You don't want the fat completely evenly distributed; the occasional little nubbin makes for a flakier end result.

Stir, using a spoon, or pulse in the yoghurt, until the mix is just combined, getting your hands in there at the end to ensure it is making a ball. Don't overwork the dough. Cover with plastic wrap and refrigerate for an hour or two before using. When ready to roll, dust with a lot of flour, or perhaps even roll between sheets of baking paper to ensure the pastry doesn't stick to your bench.

Lard Shortcrust Pastry

Makes 450 g (1 lb)

This is a very short, savoury pastry of the kind my mum made for pretty much every purpose when I was growing up. Oftentimes, even with desserts such as my great nan's apple pie (see A Right and Proper Apple Pie, page 261), an unsweetened pastry like this is just the ticket.

- 75 g (2¾ oz) lard, chilled
- 75 g (2¾ oz) butter, chilled and diced
- 300 g (10½ oz/2 cups) plain (all-purpose) flour
- generous pinch of salt
- 1–2 tablespoons iced water

Rub the lard and butter into the flour and salt with your fingertips (or pulse in a food processor) until the mixture resembles breadcrumbs. The idea is that you don't want the fats to warm too much, so don't overdo it. In fact, a slightly lumpy crumb mix is better than overworking it.

Once the fat is relatively well rubbed in, add enough water to allow you to – very gently – knead the mixture into a firm dough. Again, don't overwork it; as soon as it comes together evenly, roll it into a ball, cover with plastic wrap and allow to rest in the fridge for about 30 minutes before rolling.

Hot Water Pastry

Makes 900 g (2 lb)

This is a lovely, flavoursome pastry that lifts your pie or your pasty (see page 127) to great heights. Use it with the *Panada* (page 139), too. In the absence of duck or goose fat, you can use 100 g (3½ oz) pork lard with the butter and the result is nearly as good.

50 g (1¾ oz) pork lard

50 g (1¾ oz) goose or duck fat

100 g (3½ oz) butter, softened

600 g (1 lb 5 oz/4 cups) plain (all-purpose) flour

1½ teaspoons salt

2 free-range eggs, beaten

Combine the lard, goose fat, butter and 250 ml (8½ fl oz/1 cup) water in a saucepan and heat until the fats have melted, but don't boil.

Mix the flour and salt in a large bowl. Make a well in the centre and tip in the eggs, stirring to combine a bit. Don't be fussy about it. Recreate the well and pour in the hot water and fat mixture. Use a knife to stir well until it's too hard to mix, then get your hands in and form the dough into a nice, even ball. Wrap it in plastic or cover with a damp tea towel (dish towel) and leave it for 30 minutes or so before rolling.

Sweet Shortcrust Pastry

Makes about 650 g (1 lb 7 oz)

Sometimes it's lovely and decadent to have a delicate, sweet, rich pastry on hand. This, then, is that.

160 g (5½ oz/⅔ cup) butter, softened slightly

120 g (4½ oz) icing (confectioners') sugar, sifted

1 teaspoon vanilla extract

250 g (9 oz/1⅔ cups) plain (all-purpose) flour, sifted

2 free-range egg yolks

In a food processor, blend the butter with the sugar and vanilla until dissolved. Pulse in the flour until the mixture is crumbly, then pulse in the yolks.

Tip the mixture onto the bench and knead just until it makes a dough. Refrigerate for 30 minutes. When you need to roll it, roll between two sheets of plastic wrap (it will be quite sticky).

Pâté Brisee (Flaky Pastry)

Makes about 500 g (1 lb 2 oz)

A slightly higher butter content and a rough mixing make for a lovely, buttery but flaky pastry.

150 g (5½ oz) butter, chilled and diced

250 g (9 oz/1⅔ cups) plain (all-purpose) flour, plus extra for dusting

good pinch of salt

3–4 tablespoons ice-cold water

Rub the butter into the flour and salt or pulse it in a food processor until crumbly. Don't be fussy about it being too even; a coarser mixture makes a better pastry. Add just enough of the water to make a pliable dough. Don't overmix.

Cover with plastic wrap and leave to rest for at least half an hour before rolling. Roll out on a well-floured bench, or between sheets of baking paper to fit your tatin dish or tin, then leave in the fridge until needed.

Pizza Dough

Makes 4 thin bases

The very best pizza is made from a soft dough that is allowed to rise slowly to give it a better texture and taste – 36 hours is good. But you can knock this up in a couple of hours if you are in a hurry – and it's still good. Bake your pizza on a heavy, unglazed tile for the finest results.

540 g (1 lb 3 oz) really fine-ground plain (all-purpose) flour

7 g (¼ oz) sachet active dried yeast

3 teaspoons salt

½ teaspoon sugar

1–2 tablespoons olive oil (optional)

Combine the flour, yeast, salt and sugar in a large bowl, then make a well in the middle and add 400 ml (13½ fl oz) water (tepid, or blood temperature, if you're in a hurry).

Knead to a smooth dough for about 5 minutes, then return to a clean bowl and coat with the oil. Cover and refrigerate overnight. It will rise, but slowly. The next day, knead again to incorporate all the oil. Roll into four evenly sized balls, then place in an oiled bowl again and refrigerate until ready to use.

Home-made Pasta

Makes 300 g (10½ oz)

Once you've mastered the art of home-made egg pasta, it can be hard to go back to the packet stuff.

about 200 g (7 oz/1⅓ cups) plain (all-purpose) flour, the finer ground the better, plus extra for dusting

2 × 60 g (2 oz) free-range eggs

By machine: Place the flour in a food processor and pulse to mix. Add the eggs and pulse to combine well. Remove from the food processor and knead to a firm, smooth dough by hand, adding a little more flour or a few drops of water if necessary to balance the mixture.

By hand: Place the flour in a big volcano shape on a clean bench and crack the eggs into the centre. Mix the eggs in a circular motion to mangle, and gradually incorporate the flour from the edge into the middle. Once the mixture comes together, knead by hand to a smooth dough.

Roll out, preferably using a pasta machine, in at least four batches, to make very thin pasta sheets. Start by dusting each piece in flour, then pressing down to flatten the dough so it's easier to work with. Roll the dough several times at the largest setting, folding and pressing together between each roll. Reduce the thickness of the sheets by adjusting the machine by one notch after each roll. Use plenty of flour as you go to avoid the pasta sticking. When you get to the smallest setting that you want, always roll the pasta through twice. (On my machine, I very rarely use the narrowest setting, preferring to use the second-narrowest instead.) This double roll at the end minimises the amount of shrinkage as the dough settles after rolling. You can use these big flat sheets to make lasagne or ravioli, too.

To make angel hair or tagliatelle, use the attachments on the machine for cutting the pasta. To make pappardelle, dust the sheets lightly with flour, then fold each in half, then half again and cut into strips about 2 cm (¾ in) wide. Pull the strands apart so that they don't stick.

To make quadretti, cut the sheets into 1 cm (½ in) pappardelle, then cut into squares.

Cook immediately in a saucepan of boiling, well-salted water, or dry by draping the pasta over the handles of wooden spoons or a clean broomstick suspended between two chairs.

When you want to eat it, cook in plenty of boiling, well-salted water until still firm to the bite. Drain, but don't rinse. Serve immediately.

Flatbreads

Makes 4

We make bread and flatbread quite often, sometimes using mashed potato with the flour and no yeast, but often just using ingredients that we always have in the cupboard. This is a good-flavoured, easy bread to master.

270 g (9½ oz) plain (all-purpose) flour, plus extra for dusting

50 g (1¾ oz) plain yoghurt

¾ teaspoon baking powder

pinch of dried yeast

pinch of salt

40 g (1½ oz) butter, melted

Mix together all the ingredients, except the butter, with 150 ml (5 fl oz) water and knead well. Rest for 30 minutes on the bench. The dough may be a bit sticky and that's okay.

Knead in the butter and leave for another 30 minutes before rolling. Divide the dough into four even-sized balls. Roll out to about 22 cm (8¾ in) rounds with plenty of flour. Dry-fry in a heavy-based frying pan over a high flame for a few minutes, turning twice so that each side cooks and browns a little.

Fermented Carrots

Makes 1 kg (2lb 3 oz)

We started fermenting carrots when we had a glut, and now grow extras just to ferment! Flavours vary from batch to batch, season to season, but a little sourness, a little funk is the aim. We've adapted this from the recipe in Cornersmith's cool pickling book.

25 g (1 oz) salt

1 kg (2lb 3 oz) small carrots, well scrubbed (cut in half lengthwise if large)

2.5 cm (1 in) chunk ginger, sliced

2 medium onions, peeled and thinly sliced

2 garlic cloves, peeled and chopped

1 teaspoon turmeric

Dissolve the salt in 1 litre (34 fl oz/4 cups) water.

Place the carrots in a non-reactive container (glass works really well) with the ginger, onions and garlic. A plastic bucket is less glamorous, but also does the job nicely.

Heat a dry frying pan over a very low flame, add the turmeric and cook lightly for 30 seconds. Add this to the salty water, then pour the water over the carrots, pressing them down to ensure they're submerged. You want the carrots and onions below the surface to avoid them going mouldy. A weighted saucer on top helps, if your container is big enough.

Cover with a loose lid or cheesecloth, and leave at room temperature, out of the breeze and the sun, for 3-6 days, depending on your location and the season and your palate. Warmer climes will need less time. The carrots will start to ferment, and the brine will start to fizz a little as they go. Taste after three days, and you'll see their progress. When they're as sharp flavoured as you'd like, pop a lid on properly and store in the fridge. You can eat them whole, but we like to use them as a paste, or in smaller pieces to match cheese or cured meats. Once they're in the fridge, they should keep for three months easily.

Naan

Serves 4

These Indian-inspired breads go really well with lamb, or with dips and the like. A wood-fired pizza oven is ideal, a chargrill great, but a hot domestic grill or lightly oiled frying pan are good options too.

7 g (¼ oz) sachet active dried yeast

1 tablespoon tepid water

1 teaspoon sugar

200 g (7 oz) plain yoghurt

230 g (8 oz) plain (all-purpose) flour, plus extra for dusting

¼ teaspoon salt

melted butter, for brushing

Mix the yeast, water and sugar in a big bowl, then set aside to rest and allow the mixture to foam (this shows the yeast is alive). Whisk in the yoghurt, then stir in the flour and salt.

Knead the dough on a well-floured board for 10 minutes (or use a freestanding electric mixer fitted with the dough hook attachment and mix for 5 minutes). Cover and allow to rise for 2 hours or so. Punch down, knead for another 5 minutes, then divide the dough into six pieces. Using well-floured fingers, very gently stretch and pull the dough to form 12 cm (4¾ in) rounds. The reason you don't roll it is the same as pizza dough; you don't want to squash out all the air, so pulling and stretching has a better end result.

Cook under a super-hot grill/broiler (or try a lightly oiled frying pan or even a moderately hot barbecue chargrill plate) until brown on each side. If you're cooking it on the barbecue, turn about three times to ensure even cooking without burning the breads. Brush with a little butter and serve warm.

Garlic Naan

Heat 2 tablespoons butter with 2 sliced garlic cloves and simmer for 2 minutes. Use this to brush onto the bread once cooked.

Ricotta and Chilli Naan

150 g (5½ oz) ricotta

generous pinch of salt

1 green chilli, finely sliced

1 tablespoon chopped coriander (cilantro)

good pinch of ground cinnamon

Ricotta and Chilli Naan

Mix all of the ingredients together and spoon a little onto each piece of dough. Fold over and press the edges well to seal. Grill as above, perhaps lowering the heat if needed to ensure they cook through without burning.

Ciabatta

Makes 4 small loaves

A lot of bakers like to make a sponge: essentially a wet, yeasty mass, to help make better bread. We usually don't bother, because it's an extra step that may not make much difference to the bread we bake, which is consumed within 4 hours of baking. But, for ciabatta, which is quite a wet dough, the sponge is a useful way of hydrating some of the flour (making it absorb more water), which makes it stretchier and more likely to have those large holes and chewy texture that makes this bread so enticing. This isn't a bread for slicing for sandwiches but for tearing and dipping and using to wipe your plate clean: the ultimate compliment to both the baker and the chef.

Sponge

250 g (9 oz/1⅓ cups) bread (strong) flour

125 ml (4 fl oz/½ cup) warm water

7 g (¼ oz) sachet active dried yeast

Bread

12 g (¼ oz) salt

50 ml (1¾ fl oz) olive oil

500 g (1 lb 2 oz/3⅓ cups) bread (strong) flour, plus extra for dusting

For the sponge, mix the flour, water and yeast in a large bowl until well combined and leave to rest until doubled in size, about 30 minutes. Cover and pop into a cool spot, even the fridge, overnight.

The next day, at least 12 hours later, remove the sponge from the fridge and allow it to rise for another hour.

To make the bread, combine the salt and olive oil with 350 ml (12 fl oz) water in a freestanding electric mixer fitted with the dough hook attachment. Add the flour and the sponge, then mix on the slowest setting. Once the mixture is well combined, turn up the mixer to knead the dough for about 10 minutes, or until very stretchy. Bakers would do this with a big slap and scrape on the bench for 10 minutes and get a great texture through working it, but most home cooks find this a bit messy, strenuous and tedious.

When the dough has been well kneaded, leave it on a stupidly well-floured board or bench, keeping an eye on it as it will start to almost run off the bench as it rises. If it does spread too far, scoop up the edge and lay it back onto itself to form a bigger pile.

Preheat the oven to its maximum heat. Flour the dough well on top, then divide it into four pieces. Shape the loaves quickly using your hands by tucking in the sides to form logs, but all the while trying not to knock air out of the dough. Place these logs on two well-floured baking trays and bake for about 15 minutes, turning the trays and swapping shelves in the oven after about 8–10 minutes.

The bread should have some colour and sound hollow when tapped on the base once cooked. Cool on wire racks and serve the same day.

Yolanda's Seedy Lavosh

Makes 8

We have been privileged to work with many people at Fat Pig over the years. Some come for full-time work and stay a while, or a long while, and some are casuals that bring their enthusiasm and energy from other projects. One such casual is Yolanda, who in her real job works on wigs and costumes for television and movies. One day she brought in some of her crispbread, lavosh, which was much seedier than the one we used to make, and it instantly became a favourite. This is her recipe, and it's the nigella seeds that we suspect are what really make it stand out. Find them at good whole food stores, supermarkets or Indian grocers.

300 g (10½ oz/2 cups) plain (all-purpose) flour (bread [strong] flour is even better), plus extra for dusting

¼ teaspoon salt

½ teaspoon dried rosemary

½ teaspoon freshly ground black pepper

1½ teaspoons nigella seeds

3 teaspoons sesame seeds

1 teaspoon cornflour (cornstarch)

1 tablespoon rice flour

1 tablespoon olive oil

semolina, for dusting

Preheat the oven to 180°C (350°F).

Mix all the ingredients together with 200 ml (7 fl oz) water to make a dough, then divide it into eight pieces. Flour the bench and each piece well, and roll into a ball.

Roll out each ball of dough, either by hand on a very well floured surface, or through a pasta machine, as thin as you dare. If you're struggling, it's worth using semolina to help it roll without sticking.

Place on a baking tray lined with baking paper and bake for 10–15 minutes, or until golden, maybe even turning them over halfway through for more even cooking.

Cool and serve, perhaps with cheese, perhaps with a drink. Preferably both.

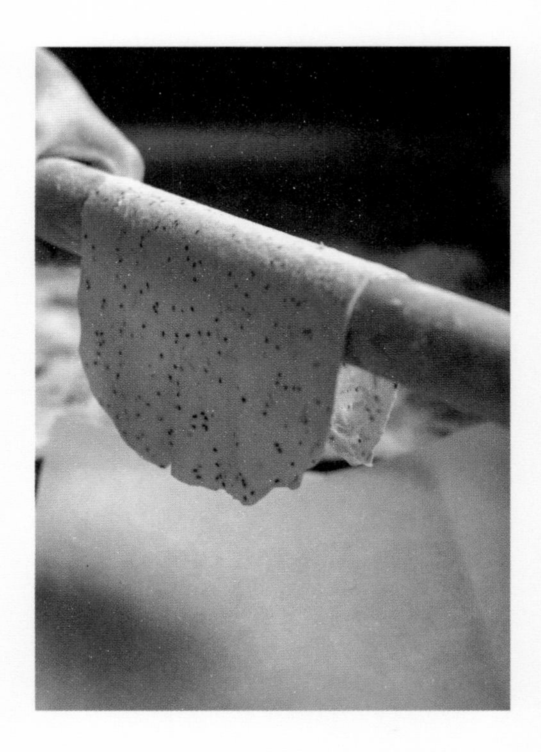

Whole Milk Ricotta and Paneer

Serves 6

Home-made ricotta and paneer are quite similar if made with whole milk (traditional ricotta is made with whey). One is crumbly, the other clumped together enough to cut and fry. Once fried, the paneer is delicious in spiced, well-cooked greens, which are called saag in Punjabi.

4 litres (135 fl oz/16 cups) full-cream (whole) milk, unhomogenised milk or whey, if you have it (for ricotta)

1 tablespoon salt

150 ml (5 fl oz) white vinegar

Put the milk or whey into a large saucepan set over a low heat and heat gently, stirring regularly to prevent it from catching on the base of the pan, until it reaches 60°C (140°F) on a cooking thermometer.

Stir in the salt and continue to heat the milk until it reaches 92°C (198°F). Do not let it boil or it denatures the protein and will prevent it from forming good curds. Remove from the heat and stir in the vinegar diluted with 200 ml (7 fl oz) water. Allow to rest for 1 minute. You will see the curds rise to the top.

Line a colander or sieve with a few layers of muslin (cheesecloth), or even a clean disposable cloth, and set it over a bowl. Use a slotted spoon to lift the curds into the colander to drain the whey, then, if you want paneer, press the resultant curds as you allow them to cool.

Pastry Cream

Makes 600 g (1 lb 5 oz)

There are countless variations on this, but I like a thick, custard-cream mix in my éclairs.

6 free-range egg yolks

85 g (3 oz/⅔ cup) icing (confectioners') sugar

100 g (3½ oz/⅔ cup) plain (all-purpose) flour, sifted

500 ml (17 fl oz/2 cups) full-cream (whole) milk

1 vanilla bean

finely grated zest of ½ lemon

100 ml (3½ fl oz) pouring (single/light) cream, lightly whipped

Mix the egg yolks and sugar in a bowl and beat until pale, thick and creamy, either by hand or with an electric mixer. Beat in the flour, a little at a time.

Heat the milk and vanilla bean until nearly boiling, then whisk in the egg mixture and return to a low heat. Whisk constantly until the mixture thickens and boils for a minute or so – it should be smooth and the flour fully cooked out.

Remove from the heat, take out the vanilla bean and add the lemon zest. (Rinse and dry the vanilla bean and pop it into a jar of caster sugar to make vanilla sugar.)

Pour this custard into a clean container, press plastic wrap onto the top and refrigerate until ready to use. To make pastry cream, whisk this set custard well until smooth, then fold in the whipped cream.

Home-made Mascarpone

Makes 500 g (1 lb 2 oz/2 cups)

Mascarpone is one of the world's most exciting creams. But often the stuff you buy isn't as good as it could be. By making it yourself, you won't have to pay exorbitant prices and will also get a better result than if you were to buy a commercial variety. You can replace the lemon juice with lime juice or vinegar, or add 1 teaspoon citric acid and a vanilla bean to the simmered cream and let it infuse for 15 minutes. Some recipes heat the cream more gently for longer (92°C/198°F for 10 minutes), but I find this quick and easy version works just as well.

600 ml (20½ fl oz) pouring (single/light) cream

1 tablespoon freshly squeezed lemon juice, strained (you can also use ¼ teaspoon tartaric acid dissolved in 1 tablespoon water, or 1 tablespoon white vinegar instead)

Put the cream in a saucepan over a really high heat. Bring to a simmer, add the lemon juice and cook for 1 minute. Remove from the heat and allow to cool. You can even cool it overnight in the fridge at this stage. Line a fine-mesh sieve with a piece of muslin (cheesecloth) and drain the cream over a clean bowl, refrigerating overnight until firm. Discard the liquid. The solids trapped in the cloth are your mascarpone, ready to flavour and sweeten if you desire, or just serve it as you would a rich cream.

Crêpes

Makes 8–10 small crêpes

There's only one place to toss a crêpe thick enough to be tossed, said 1950s British food writer Fanny Cradock: into the bin. I agree, because a thick crêpe is a pancake, and a thin crêpe is a work of art. When you start out, however, thicker crêpes are easier to master.

250 ml (8½ fl oz/1 cup) full-cream (whole) milk

1 tablespoon caster (superfine) sugar (omit for savoury crêpes)

2 free-range eggs

¼ teaspoon salt

90 g (3 oz) plain (all-purpose) flour, sifted

20 g (¾ oz) butter, melted, plus extra for brushing

2 teaspoons lemon zest, finely grated (omit for savoury crêpes)

Blend the milk, sugar, eggs and salt in a food processor. With the motor running, add the flour, a spoon at a time, until just smooth. Pulse in the melted butter, then add the zest and leave to rest in the fridge for 30 minutes.

Heat an 18 cm (7 in) crêpe pan or non-stick frying pan over a medium-high heat. Brush with a hint of melted butter and ladle just enough batter into the pan to thinly coat the base. Twist your wrist to swirl the mixture just once around the pan as you pour in the batter. When the base is light brown, use a spatula to turn the crêpe over and cook the other side. As a rule, the first crêpe sticks and buggers up. It looks messy, but is a bonus one for the cook to eat. Cook all the crêpes, laying one on top of another on a plate. Cover with foil and keep warm.

Note

When you first learn how to make crêpes, you may want to add extra flour (about 1–2 tablespoons). This recipe makes beautifully delicate crêpes but they can be tricky to turn for the novice. Once you're in the groove, it's much quicker to pump them out if you have two pans on the go at the same time.

Outro

A year on a farm seems a long time when seen in advance. Like having kids, though, you suddenly discover that the minutes can pass slowly, and yet the years skid by surprisingly fast. It's eight years now since we bought this patch of dirt we call Fat Pig Farm, and in many ways it feels like we've only just begun.

The changes on the land are visible and tangible. Birdlife is returning as we allow more trees to flourish. Frogs, including the delightful banjo frog, or pobblebonk, named after its banjo-like 'plunk' call, seem more bountiful on the dams now than when we arrived. There's more diversity, within the ground and above it, than there was even two years ago. Are we doing our job properly? That's for others, years into the future, to judge.

There are clues to the changes. As we pace this land, we feel the softness, or not, of the soil beneath our feet. We can sense the cover of grass in more ways than just by sight. Good pasture has a different scent. A different sound. A different feel. I've spent over a decade traipsing the soil in southern Tasmania, counting rainbows, tending gardens, growing food, husbanding animals and discovering the true flavour of ingredients.

And what I've learned is that a good, simple, fresh raspberry plucked from the cane at perfect ripeness is a thing of incomparable joy. A carrot, the humble carrot, can be brilliant unadorned, and a good one is unrecognisable from shop-bought in all but sight. Milk, straight from a cow that foraged on a lush mix of grass, is as marvellous – and as fleeting – as the best plonk.

I've learned that the heart of good cooking is inseparable from place and season. If a dish represents the soul and the mood of the cook, then the ingredients represent the true nature of the farmer. You can tell how much care a grower takes by the flavour of the food they produce. We are very lucky to live where we do, in the community we share, making a go of what we consider the noble arts: growing, cooking and serving food. We hope to inspire others to care about what they eat. To perhaps even grow some of what they serve for dinner, or at least thank, in person, the farmer who has brought not only sustenance, but joy to their table.

Growing food, rearing animals, welcoming and cooking for strangers (the last two of which are the very definition of hospitality) has humbled us. It has taught us patience. It has taught us the virtue of true friends, of honest work, of sometimes grim, sometimes exhilarating, always rewarding labour. Our job, at its heart, is to make people happy. We do this by transforming sunlight, soil, air and water into crops, then serving them at our table. This seemingly simple, yet surprisingly complex act stimulates our minds, hardens our bodies, fortifies our souls and lifts our spirits. It's our hope that others find the same delight by taking on some of the same ideas for their own table. It's through food, its production and its consumption, that we can all share in the bounty and pleasure of the commons.

Index

D

E

F

G

H

Q

R

S

T

V

W

Y

Z

Thank You

At Fat Pig Farm, we can only do what we do because of the help we get from so many people. We're so grateful to key people, past and present, who have brought their brilliant skills and love of produce to the restaurant, farm and garden.

In particular, they include:

Kellie McChesney
Phil O'Donnell
Jonathan Cooper
Zara Trihey
Nadia Danti
Michelle Crawford
Rob Cartledge
Seona Moss
Mike Layfield
Brett Clifford
Georgie Moon
Emma McPhee
Cassy Faux
Fin Fagan
Jane Herring
Jo Duffy
Juan David Ramirez Velasquez
Rowan Jordan
Meg Lobb
Urshula Leung
Noona Auderset
Megan Helmer
Junaidi Susantio
Emma Harley

The book is the result of the dedication of the team at Hardie Grant, most notably my publisher Jane Willson, whose persistence and vision drove us all to greater heights. Andrea O'Connor edited with panache, Evi O. Studio did a brilliant job on design, and project editor Anna Collett kept us all herded better even than the most persistent and hardworking kelpie. Alan Benson, my mate and photographer, captured the farm in all weather, as well as the deliciousness on the plate. I couldn't ask for a better friend or collaborator. Kellie McChesney and Michelle Crawford did a fabulous job cooking the food, and Luke Burgess styled with flair.

While it is a team effort, the farm, the restaurant, this book and the life we have created is the result of the dedication of one person above all else. Sadie Chrestman keeps me sane when all else doesn't, milks, and feeds pigs when I can't, weeds like a demon, and fills our lives with joy.

About the Author

Matthew Evans and his partner Sadie Chrestman are the co-owners of Fat Pig Farm, a 70-acre mixed holding in Southern Tasmania, where they grow the food for their on-farm restaurant. A chef by trade, Matthew has fronted six series of *Gourmet Farmer* on SBS, along with documentaries *What's the Catch* and *For the Love of Meat*. For the last two decades, he's written for magazines, newspapers and guide books and is the author of a dozen books on food, as well as two memoirs.

Published in 2019 by Hardie Grant Books, an imprint of Hardie Grant Publishing

Hardie Grant Books (Melbourne)
Building 1, 658 Church Street
Richmond, Victoria 3121

Hardie Grant Books (London)
5th & 6th Floors
52–54 Southwark Street
London SE1 1UN

hardiegrantbooks.com

A catalogue record for this book is available from the National Library of Australia

The Commons
ISBN 978 1 74379 539 2

10 9 8 7 6 5 4 3 2

Publishing Director: Jane Willson
Project Editor: Anna Collett
Editor: Andrea O'Connor @ Asterisk & Octopus
Editorial Assistant: Stephanie McClelland
Design Manager: Jessica Lowe
Designers: Evi-O. Studio | Evi O & Rosie Whelan
Photographer: Alan Benson
Styling/Props: Luke Burgess, Leesa O'Reilly
Home Economists: Kellie McChesney, Michelle Crawford
Production Manager: Todd Rechner
Production Coordinator: Mietta Yans

Colour reproduction by Splitting Image Colour Studio
Printed in China by Leo Paper Products LTD.